GW00506918

John Holt

Volumes of the *Continuum Library of Educational Thought* include:

John Holt

ROLAND MEIGHAN

Continuum Library of Educational Thought
Series Editor: Richard Bailey
Volume 5

continuum

Continuum International Publishing Group

The Tower Building
11 York Road
London
SE1 7NX

80 Maiden Lane
Suite 704
New York
NY 10038

www.continuumbooks.com

British Library Cataloguing-in-Publication Data
A catalogue record for this book is available from the British Library.

ISBN: 0-8264-8404-2 (hardcover)
ISBN: 978-0-8264-8404-8 (hardcover)

Library of Congress Cataloging-in-Publication Data
Meighan, Roland.
John Holt / Roland Meighan.
p.   cm.
Includes bibliographical references and index.
ISBN-13: 978-0-8264-8404-8 (hardcover)
ISBN-10: 0-8264-8404-2 (hardcover)
1. Holt, John Caldwell, 1923–1985.   2. Educators–United States–Biography.
3. Home schooling–United States.   4. Educational change–United States.
I. Title.

LA2317.H645M45   2007
370.92–dc22
2007018464

Typeset by Aptara Ltd.
Printed and bound in Great Britain by Biddles Ltd, King Lynn, Norfolk

Contents

Series Editor's Preface

Education is sometimes presented as an essentially practical activity. It is, it seems, about teaching and learning, curriculum and what goes on in schools. It is about achieving certain ends, using certain methods, and these ends and methods are often prescribed for teachers, whose duty it is to deliver them with vigor and fidelity. With such a clear purpose, what is the value of theory?

Recent years have seen politicians and policy-makers in different countries explicitly denying *any* value or need for educational theory. A clue to why this might be is offered by a remarkable comment by a British Secretary of State for Education in the 1990s: 'having any ideas about how children learn, or develop, or feel, should be seen as subversive activity'. This pithy phrase captures the problem with theory: it subverts, challenges, and undermines the very assumptions on which the practice of education is based.

Educational theorists, then, are troublemakers in the realm of ideas. They pose a threat to the *status quo* and lead us to question the common sense presumptions of educational practices. But this is precisely what they should do because the seemingly simple language of schools and schooling hides numerous contestable concepts that in their different usages reflect fundamental disagreements about the aims, values, and activities of education.

Implicit within the *Continuum Library of Educational Thought* is an assertion that theories and theorizing are vitally important for education. By gathering together the ideas of some of the most influential, important and interesting educational thinkers, from the Ancient Greeks to contemporary scholars, the series has the ambitious task of providing an accessible yet authoritative resource for a generation of students and practitioners. Volumes within the series are written by acknowledged leaders in the field, who were selected both for their scholarship and their ability to make often complex ideas accessible to a diverse audience.

It will always be possible to question the list of key thinkers that are represented in this series. Some may question the inclusion of certain thinkers;

some may disagree with the exclusion of others. That is inevitably going to be the case. There is no suggestion that the list of thinkers represented within the *Continuum Library of Educational Thought* is in any way definitive. What is incontestable is that these thinkers have fascinating ideas about education and, that taken together, the *Library* can act as a powerful source of information and inspiration for those committed to the study of education.

Richard Bailey
Roehampton University, London

Foreword

John Holt is a rare writer about education because he brought about changes not only in schools but also in our homes. Holt was a major influence on the school reform movement of the 1960s and 1970s, and then, when he decided most people did not want schools to change in the progressive, learner-centered ways he advocated, he became a major influence on the modern homeschooling movement. Equally remarkably for someone working in the field of education, Holt wrote all his books in a deliberately accessible style for the general public, and he did this as an independent researcher, without affiliation to, or the support of, any university or public or private institution. When *How Children Fail* became a national best-seller in 1964, Holt was encouraged by a friend to enter the world of academia instead of becoming an independent critic. Holt responded, in a letter quoted in *A Life Worth Living: Selected Letters of John Holt* (Ohio State University Press, 1992):

> I am trying to find out why the capacity of so many children for perceiving, and learning, and thinking, declines so rapidly as they grow older, and what we could do to prevent this from happening . . . I am very firmly convinced that a university tie would hinder my work far more than it would help it ... I can think of a number of projects that I have carried out in past years, in my own classes or with individual children. From these I have learned a great deal. None of them would have been considered a research project as a university ordinarily understands the word . . . I explore the intelligence of children by creating situations and then seeing how they respond to them and what they make of them. I am truly exploring, and an explorer does not know, when he starts into a bit of unknown country, what he is going to find there. But this is not how most of what passes for educational research is done, or how research proposals are written up.
>
> . . . For the time being, it [working for a university] seems a matter of spending a large part of my time doing things their way in the hope that

they will allow me to spend some of my time doing things my way. I can't
see it; life is too short, and I believe that I can learn far more and even
have more influence working as I am.

Holt's clear-headed vision about his work in this letter shows an almost pre-
scient knowledge of his later transformations of thought and opinion as a
public intellectual, writer on education, school reformer, political activist,
and a founder of the homeschooling movement. His independence of
thought and descriptions about not just the techniques but the emotions
attached to teaching and learning continue to surprise readers, as well as
influence parents to homeschool their children. His books have now been
translated into over 20 languages, and they continue to generate adherents
and controversy.

For instance, Holt's vision of homeschooling, or 'unschooling' as he preferred to call it in the early years of the movement, was not about doing
school at home with one's siblings and parents. Instead, it was about learning in and outside the home, in places and with people that do not resemble
school at all. Holt viewed learning as an abundant, natural, human endeavor
that gets warped or turned off by imposing years of unasked-for teaching
upon the learner. He envisioned not just families but entire communities
becoming places for lifelong learning. Indeed, Holt's writing continues to
inspire people to create cooperative learning centers and develop other
forms of community-based activities for children and adults, defying the
charge leveled against homeschoolers that they are interested only in their
own children and circumstances. However, to use a current analogy from the
world of high technology, most educators refuse to ackowledge Holt's 'open
source' approach to education and insist on their 'proprietary' approach to
making children learn what they think they need to know, month by month,
year by year. Often it seems that these rival visions of education are irrecon-
cilable. Fortunately, Roland Meighan has written this wonderful exposition
of John Holt's work that provides us with a sensitive understanding of how
these visions of education can indeed be reconciled.

Meighan summarizes Holt's work in clear prose that Holt himself would
have enjoyed, and Meighan puts Holt's work in the context of our current
times. Most professional educators and politicians dismiss Holt's work as
'romantic' and impractical because of the radical changes it could make to
compulsory schooling. However, as Meighan points out, Holt's ideas about
teaching and learning are important and practical, and they continue to
be implemented and adapted by a variety of homeschooling parents and
independent alternative schools. Read this book to learn not only about
John Holt's work but also about what you can do in your own life to person-
alize education and make it meaningful not just to yourself but for others

as well. In this age of regressive, formulaic compulsory schooling, Roland Meighan's book shows us how Holt's work is truly 'radical' – that is, it goes back to the root of education – and how people outside the school system can influence and change education in ways that reformers inside the school system cannot.

Patrick Farenga
Formerly of John Holt Associates and
Growing Without Schooling magazine for over 24 years.
Co-author of *Teach Your Own: The John Holt Book of Homeschooling* (Perseus, 2003)

Part 1

Intellectual Biography

Chapter 1

Becoming a Radical

There was little in the first part of John Holt's life to indicate the fame that was to overtake him later. He was born in 1923 in New York City, the eldest of three children, and grew up in the New England area of the USA. His two sisters, Jane and Susan, married to become Jane Pitcher and Susan Bontecou and had families – one had five children and the other six – but John remained single. This was not of his choosing, he used to explain, for he was open to the idea of marriage, but it just never happened.

He died of cancer in 1985 aged 62. By that time he had written ten books with memorable and challenging titles and even more memorable and challenging contents. His work had been translated into 14 languages. His first two books sold over a million copies and became some of the best-read books on education ever produced. Professor Ted Wragg of Exeter University noted in conversation with me that of all the books he ever recommended on education, John Holt's were the most read and appreciated, and caused the most debate and feedback.

Holt was not impressed by the schools and colleges he attended, even though they were 'good' schools and colleges for the wealthy and 'successful', and he preferred not to even name them. All the important things that he knew, had not been learned in these institutions, he declared, so why give them any credit? I can sympathize with Holt here, since I remember trying to explain to relatives and others that the grammar school for boys I attended in my youth was just an endurance test and that my real education was taking place in my family, my neighborhood, the church, the youth club and the local public library. My observations stimulated little comment or discussion other than vague accusations of ingratitude, so I soon learned to keep my thoughts to myself.

During the Second World War, Holt served as a commissioned officer on a submarine in the Pacific after graduation from college in 1943. He wrote that he learned many lessons about teamwork and cooperation while living on a submarine. The submarine sank two ships in the Java Sea before it was itself damaged by a bomb.

After the destruction of Hiroshima by an atomic bomb, Holt concluded that the devastation of the world was only a matter of time unless good people took action. So, he worked in the peace movement for the World Federalist Movement in New York City for six years, giving hundreds of lectures and traveling to Europe and elsewhere. After a further year touring Europe, he returned to the USA and visited one of his sisters in Santa Fe. He told her he was thinking of becoming a farmer, but her response was that he was so good with her children, he should consider teaching.

Holt was not keen, but his sister persisted and persuaded him to visit Rocky Mountain School near Aspen, which had just opened, and since the school intended to grow its own food, he could learn farming there. He worked as a volunteer until a regular teacher left and he filled the vacancy. He worked mostly with the 'bad' students, and it was from these that he learned most about the challenges of teaching. So, without the persuasive powers of his sister, Holt might have remained in obscurity for the rest of his life.

During this time, he began to write a series of letters to various friends containing his observations about teaching and learning. John's own self-image was that of 'problem solver', so having taken up teaching he set about solving the various problems he was now encountering. Later, these became part of the text of his first book, *How Children Fail*.

Four years later, aged 34, he moved to Boston. The move came about more or less by accident. He had been invited to look after a friend's apartment while the friend was away for a year. Holt found Boston to his liking and he lived there for the rest of his life. A Boston school hired him to teach, but his insistence that testing was harmful to learning was not welcomed and he was asked to leave.

At two other schools, his ideas were not welcomed either, and each time he was asked to leave. Schools were just a means to an end, Holt's declared, and when people accused him of deserting schools and teachers, he responded that he never identified with them in the first place. He worked in them to develop answers to questions about learning and children, not because he ever believed in them.

How Children Fail became a best-seller more or less by accident. The first print run was not doing too well, but Pitman Publishing, being rather short of titles, decided to keep it on their list for a little longer. In the meantime, Holt wrote a letter to Eliot Fremont-Smith, book reviewer of the *New York Times*. Fremont-Smith read the book and wrote a front-page endorsement of this new book ('possibly the most penetrating and probably the most eloquent book on education to be published in recent years . . . '), and sales soared. The next month it sold 2,000 copies. In 1966 Holt's second book, *How Children Learn*, was in print and soon Holt became something of a celebrity, giving lectures, speeches, and radio and television interviews. His writing was eventually translated into 14 different languages as he developed an international reputation for his radical ideas on education in general, and schools in particular.

As Mel Allen remarked in his piece on John Holt for *Yankee* magazine in December 1981, Holt's writing style was very accessible, in contrast to most of the output on schools and education. So Holt soon became one of the few writers to reach the mass audiences, and his work was taken up in the UK by Penguin Books with great success.

Holt found common cause with A.S. Neill, founder of Summerhill School, and they met first in 1965. Their common ground began with the proposition that children can be trusted to learn about their world with far less adult interference than is commonly believed. Shortly before Neill died, in 1973, Holt visited Summerhill again, when they talked as much about death, since Neill was ailing, as about education. Holt was not to know that his own death was not too far away – 12 years away, in fact.

Holt also spent time with Ivan Illich. In 1969 he was invited to be involved in seminars in Cuernavaca, Mexico, and spent two weeks there working with Illich, and this pattern was repeated for another four years. Illich had developed the view that schools and schooling were a disastrous idea in poor countries and locked them more deeply in poverty, dependency and helplessness. Following this concern, Illich became interested in the whole effect of schooling in rich countries too, and Holt was one of a number of people invited to contribute to the seminars. But the purpose, Holt decided, was more of a learning exchange than anything formal, as the visitors sought to gain from Illich's ideas and Illich sought to pick their brains.

One irony Holt noted was that for all his national and international reputation as an educational commentator, his adopted city of Boston ignored his existence: 'Of the 24 years I have lived in Boston, I've been known as a kind of educational expert for 17 of them. In those 17 years only one person connected with the Boston school system has ever talked to me.' This person turned out to be a teacher of remedial mathematics to Hispanic high-school youngsters, who reported later that Holt's suggestions had been very helpful to him.

But Holt's relationship with teachers in general fluctuated. While he was talking about classrooms and what might be done to make them more effective learning environments, he was apparently on their side. But when he talked about the need to go way beyond such damage limitation and recycle schools into learner-managed places, he lost their sympathy. Teachers, he observed, were not very brave people, and certainly not brave enough to engage in radical changes. At first he thought 75 per cent of teachers were with him, then perhaps 50 per cent, then, later still, 25 per cent. In the end, he concluded that the figure was more like 2 or even 1 per cent.

By 1981, the forces of regressive education in the USA began to reassert themselves with slogans such as 'Back to the Basics'. Much the same thing happened in the UK. Holt reluctantly began to conclude that regressive attitudes might even make up the majority view. 'Very few people, inside the schools or out, were willing to support or even tolerate giving more freedom, choice and self-direction to children' (*Teach your Own*, p. 4). Freedom had not been treated as a serious proposition but as a possible motivational device. When it did not bring quick results it was soon discredited. This led Holt to write two books with a different message, *Escape from Childhood* and *Instead of Education*, where he explored the uncomfortable idea that most adults in the USA distrust and rather dislike most children, sometimes even their own. He proposed that people whose lives are hard or boring or painful or meaningless – people who suffer – tend to resent those who seem to suffer less than they do, and will make them suffer too if they can. People in chains with no apparent hope of losing them want to put chains on others. The great majority of boring, regimented schools were doing exactly what most people wanted them to do: Teach children about Reality; Teach them that Life Is No Picnic; Teach them to Shut Up and Do What You're Told.

John Holt was not impressed. He said of such schools that they demonstrated that a school based on such a view was not just a good idea gone wrong, but a bad idea from the start. He concluded that 'Back to the Basics' was really code for 'No More Fun and Games in School'. Most adults in the USA, he observed, do not care all that much about reading, since they read little themselves. Like most Americans, young or old, they spend much of their leisure time watching TV. What they want their children to learn is how to *work* – but not good and skillful work they can be proud of. Few have that kind of work themselves, or ever expect to. They want their children, when their time comes, to be able and willing to hold down full-time unpleasant jobs of their own. The best way to get them ready to do this is to make school as much like a full-time, unpleasant job as possible.

This was not just a working-class attitude, he noted. A middle-class couple who had transferred their son to the school Holt was teaching in were pleased that there had been a great improvement in both their son's studies and his behavior, but expressed some anxiety about how much fun he was having in school. After all, he was going to have to spend the rest of his life doing things he did not like, and he might as well start getting used to it.

The reason for these bleak attitudes was not cruelty or mean-spiritedness, but *fatalism*. In their view, this was how the world was, and there was little chance of its changing for the better. In addition, such people had developed faith in violence as a way to solve problems, despite the evidence of its failure. While such parents were in a majority, Holt concluded, any radical school reform was doomed.

Holt saw the effect of compulsory schooling on teachers as demeaning. Since compulsory school attendance laws force teachers to do custodial work anyway, real teaching becomes more and more difficult. If you add to this the requirement to implement a regressive vision of education of the 'No More Fun in Schools' variety, teaching increasingly becomes a grim and repressive task. It would be in the teachers' best interests to do away with compulsion and establish instead what has been called elsewhere the 'Invitational School'.

His most fervent supporters turned out to be parents and, when he realized this, he began to work with the emerging home-based education movement, referred to in the USA as homeschooling. As regressive ideas came back into fashion, John Holt decided to work with the minority of more optimistic parents who wanted something different. At first this was with groups who were active in setting up small alternative schools. These usually struggled because of the problems of finance.

But some of these parents had begun to educate their children at home and needed support. Therefore, John Holt established a service organization called Growing Without Schooling. Home-based education became the focus of his writing and activity. His work, and the work of many others, has borne fruit. Today, over one million families in the USA are engaged in home-based education. Home-based education in the USA has its own research journal, its own publishing house and a considerable range of commercial publications and services.

Part 2

Critical Exposition of John Holt's Work

Chapter 2

Overview

It was said of John Holt that even if his writing had not been so good, he certainly knew how to craft an interesting book title! Here are the ten titles in order:

How Children Fail (1964)
How Children Learn (1967)
The Underachieving School (1970)
What Do I Do Monday? (1970)
Freedom and Beyond (1972)
Escape from Childhood (1975)
Instead of Education (1976)
Never Too Late (1979)
Teach Your Own (1981)
Learning All the Time (1989).

And finally, there was the periodical entitled

Growing Without Schooling (1977 onwards).

The titles of his books indicate a developing theme: a critical review of schools in the USA as they existed in the 1960s and 1970s that gradually gave way to a growing disenchantment with any efforts to change them. Finally, Holt concluded they would not change, and indeed could not, given their basic coercive and impositional task. To change in any fundamental way, they would have to become invitational and give up on compulsion. They would have to be completely recycled. Schools, as Holt put it, were mostly in the prison business, for their prime task was custodial. To be more in the education business they would have to adopt the model of the public library and become invitational.

Holt's perceptions of schooling became more and more negative over time. In *The Underachieving School*, he began to argue that schooling was a kind of child abuse, but also an abuse of teachers. Teachers also suffer from the school attendance laws, Holt argues, because they are diverted from educational matters into being school prison guards and school police. The primary function of teaching becomes corrupted. Coaching learners gives way to the requirement to coerce. The results are that people who go into teaching full of hope and good intentions gradually become used to thinking of themselves as having the role of police and of the children as their natural enemies. It becomes no more possible to have open, friendly and mutually helpful relationships between most teachers and students than it is between most prison guards and prison convicts – and for exactly the same reasons.

People find it hard to believe that order will be maintained without compulsion, yet Holt observed that in the Boston Public Library he saw a great many students of all backgrounds behaving just as reasonably, sensibly and considerately as everybody else. A key difference was that they were there by choice and could leave whenever they wanted.

People protest that schools are compulsory to protect civil rights, to serve an 'entitlement' to education. Holt said that this had had some credibility in the past in preventing children from being used as cheap labor. But times change, and the market for child labor is hardly an issue – and, in any case, if protection is needed, it can be covered by child employment and child abuse laws.

But, Holt states, compulsory schooling is now the main form of child abuse, and children need protection from it. School is an abuse of human rights, an idea explored in Holt's book *Escape from Childhood*. In a democracy, being put into a custodial situation is only permitted if an offence has been committed and proved, or evidence can be presented that this is likely to be proved in a properly conducted hearing – 'due process'. Holt asks what *offense* children have committed to be put into school custody. They are young and have huge gaps in their knowledge and understanding, but these are not offenses against society and its rules, as are theft, murder and rape.

Holt is not impressed by the teachers who agree to do this work. In *The Underachieving School,* teachers are put under the microscope. Most new teachers are selected on the basis of their success in a system that stresses competitive examinations and the rote learning of disconnected facts. It is no surprise that they usually carry this method forward into their own teaching. Moreover, teachers are mostly recruited from a similar background. The teachers come from predominately non-intellectual or even anti-intellectual lower-middle-class backgrounds, and they look on education very much as another branch of the civil service. It is a safe, secure, and respectable way to move a rung or two from the bottom of the socio-economic ladder. Teachers, historically, were never a profession in the traditional mold of 'occupations fit for the younger sons of the gentry'. The four traditional professions were medicine, law, the clergy and the military. Teachers were seen originally as part of the servant class, and in large houses were accommodated and ate with the servants.

The result of teachers being members of qualifying associations rather than of a profession is, Holt noted, the production of cohorts of dull teachers prone to overrate order, anxiously sensitive to their own authority and status, convinced that their message of 'study hard and you can be like me' has widespread appeal to the young. What could an appeal to give children more freedom possibly mean to such teachers, who have never been free themselves? Holt concludes that city schools are bound to fail because they are full of such teachers. It was observations like these that led to Holt being seen not just as a critic of schools and education, but as a 'social critic' and a 'public intellectual' interested in much more than just school reform.

At the same time as Holt was writing, there were others who were writing critical books and articles on contemporary schooling in the USA. Holt knew these writers, and they drew some inspiration from each other. Goodman produced his indictment of the system in a book entitled *Compulsory Miseducation* in which he described the institution of schooling as a mass superstition based on the fallacy that education can only be achieved by organizing such places as schools and compelling the young to attend them. On the contrary, he declared, subjecting young people to institutionalized learning stunts and distorts their natural intellectual development, makes them hostile to the very idea of education as open enquiry, and finally turns out regimented, competitive citizens likely only to aggravate our current social ills.

In 1969, Neil Postman and Charles Weingartner published their book *Teaching as a Subversive Activity*, in which they proposed a different kind of teacher who enabled the young to develop questioning attitudes and to face the challenges of a rapidly changing society. In the same year Herbert Kohl produced his work *The Open Classroom*, advocating the replacement of the authoritarian classroom with a democratic alternative, the open classroom with learner-managed learning rather than teacher-managed learning. Then there was the work of Ivan Illich in books like *Deschooling Society* (1971) and *Alternatives to Schooling* (1972). Illich's writings were concerned not just with schools but with a wide variety of social institutions. He argued for 'convivial' institutions but found mostly 'coercive' ones instead. Such institutions deprive people of the possibility of growing as independent human beings.

A book that drew inspiration from Illich is Everett Reimer's *School Is Dead*, published in 1971, in which Reimer called for a serious consideration of alternatives in education: alternative content, organization and finance, and an alternative view of education itself. He saw education, as found in schools, as a process of enslavement and dependence that needed to give way to the education of free humans capable of mastering technology for good rather than resigned to mere cycles of competitive consumption.

It is easy to see why the mass media lumped these and other writers together under the general label of 'Deschoolers', but the general label distorted the complexity of their position. Some did want to do away with schools, others to recycle them and yet others to transform them into convivial or democratic places.

Holt himself moved across these positions. At first he thought schools could be transformed. For example, he worked with Don Glines, currently director of Educational Futures Projects, Sacramento, California, during the late 1960s and early 1970s, running workshops where Holt would analyze what was wrong with schools and Glines would go on to suggest practical changes to remedy these failings from his experience as director of the Wilson Campus School in Mankato, Minnesota (described in Meighan's *Comparing Learning Systems*, 2005). At their last workshop together, Holt said to Glines:

> Don, good luck if you continue to pursue changing the public schools, but I now see it as impossible. The best way I can help kids is to show them how to escape schooling. I will not do any more workshops for public school people, but will focus on such as home-based education, and private schools that might be recycled into smaller parent-led and learner-managed places, and help a few like yourself in the public area who understand how school are like jails.

Glines continued to work with people like Wayne Jennings, Lloyd Trump, Dwight Allen, Ed Pino and others who remained optimistic and who did, for a time, effect some changes. Glines commented, 'Then Reagan got elected – the right wing got control, uniformity ruled – and schooling is now *worse* than it has *ever* been in the US.'

Later, Holt proposed that schools be done away with altogether. Home-based educators have the opportunity to pursue real learning in the real world, or 'lifeschool'. This gives them an advantage over almost all schools, for even in 'free' or alternative schools there is too much tendency to defer to what conventional schools do by taking learners away from the great richness and variety of the real world and replacing it with an artificial and contrived learning environment. As one parent put it, her daughter lived in a world of marvelous abundance where her resources were unlimited. She had not been 'socialized' by school to think that education is a supply of scarce knowledge controlled by teachers and to be competed for by controlled children.

Another family stressed to Holt the incidental learning acquired from everyday events. They planned a special 'educational' field trip once a week as part of their learning program. These were fun and not without value, but the phoniness and rigidity of their ritual finally got to the family and they stopped doing it as a routine. The weekly trips to the town to shop, use the library, the bank, the post office and other local facilities became more valued as a result.

This led Holt to suggest that the country club remodeled as a family club would be a better expenditure of public money than schools. There would be no curriculum, just facilities and opportunities for meeting, living and doing things. As one parent observed to Holt, any young person who has been to the usual type of school knows that school is only a euphemism for a children's day prison.

Holt emphasizes the idea that play is serious for learners; in effect, it is young children's *work*. Included are several accounts from families relating to this theme. This leads into one of John Holt's main themes, that of learning without teaching. Learning is defined in a quite straightforward way as 'finding out'. He suggests that it may wound us a little to realize that children can often get along very well as learners without adult help and that if they need it, they will ask for it.

He refers back to his proposition in *How Children Fail*, that it is fear, boredom and the confusion of having constantly to manipulate meaningless words and symbols that make children stupid, and adds a further insight: that others have taken control of their minds. It is being taught, in the sense of being trained like circus animals to do tricks on demand, that has made them stupid (at least in school). The most important question any thinking creature can ask itself, Holt proposed, is 'What is worth thinking about?' When we deny the right of people to decide for themselves, when we try to control what people must attend to and think about, we make people less observant, resourceful and adaptive – in a word, less intelligent; in a blunter word, more stupid, he concludes.

Alongside his interest in schools and the education system, John Holt developed his own interest and competence in music. When I met him at the railway station in Birmingham in 1982 he arrived in the company of his cello. This somewhat unusual piece of luggage signaled the priority he gave to his music in the later years of his life. In between his speaking engagements he would return to our house and settle down to play.

He began to play the flute in his early thirties. A few years later he switched to the cello, playing it for a couple of years. Rarely do adults who have never played take up an instrument in middle age, and least of all a bowed string instrument such as a cello, since the common assumption is that it is too hard to learn later in life. At the age of 50, Holt took up the cello once more, having stopped playing for a while following the success of his first book. He decided to write up his experiences in the hope that his story might encourage other people, who may have been told that they were too old to begin to play a musical instrument. Becoming a skillful musician now became the most important remaining task of his life, and he became proficient enough to play in local chamber orchestras.

This book that recorded Holt's experiences of becoming a musician was also a significant work about education, about teaching, especially self-teaching, and also learning, especially learner-managed learning. *Never Too Late* is especially about the teaching of music.

Since his parents were quite well off, Holt had a comfortable life when young. As an adult, he chose to live simply with very little money and selected work he believed in, initially in the peace movement. His modest lifestyle meant that he had few worries about money. The fact that he did not marry was to become a contributory factor. He explains that this was not of his choosing. Marriage just never happened. Thus, he met a girl he liked very much and went out with, but in the end she found someone else (*Never Too Late*, p. 87).

He had sufficient money, therefore, to be able to explore, enjoy and make music. But his joy in music led him to identify a public need to make musical resources available to people with little money.

From 1966 to 1973, Holt was constantly on the road lecturing and broadcasting in his work for school reform. In between times he continued his writing. He linked up with Ivan Illich and was influenced by the idea of deinstitutionalization. Institutions had taken over people's lives. People had come to believe that anything and everything they wanted or needed could only be supplied by some complicated, large, expensive and run-from-the-top organization. Holt favored the idea that people could act directly and cooperatively to satisfy their needs. Learning the cello now seemed an integral part of that concern, so he took it up again in 1973. As we shall see in Chapter 10, in his reflections on his own learning of the cello, recounted in *Never Too Late*, many of Holt's ideas about effective learning are reinforced.

The next ten chapters consider each of Holt's books in turn. There is some repetition in these accounts since Holt revisited, recycled and revised his ideas book by book. Holt himself would probably have been philosophical about this, declaring that new or radical ideas had to become familiar through repetition and restatement, and that good ideas were worth repeating anyway.

Chapter 3

How Children Fail

The work of John Holt came to my notice in a rather unusual way. My first partner came home from her school with a copy of *How Children Fail* – in 1968, as I recall. Shirley was a teacher of the younger children at one of the few primary schools in the English Midlands ever to try to take the Plowden Report's ideas at all seriously, much to the incredulity of the other schools in the area. (The Plowden Report was the 1967 Report of the Central Advisory Council for Education on primary education in England and Wales, which advocated child-centered approaches to teaching.) Wherever the 'Plowden revolution' was later alleged to have taken place, I can report with some confidence that it was *not* in the Midlands, since I and my colleagues were in and out of the region's primary schools with our students on a regular basis. Here the 'Dick Turpin' highwayman approach continued to hold sway: 'stand and deliver'. Indeed, research such as the ORACLE project from the University of Leicester indicates that it hardly took place anywhere, despite the assertions of misinformed tabloid journalists based on a few anecdotes – some rare but true, others rare and only partly true, and others invented.

The headteacher had asked all the teachers on the staff to read *How Children Fail* in preparation for a staff meeting to reflect on the work of the school in the light of John Holt's ideas. So Shirley read it and then I read it and then we faced up to it: what Holt had to say squared uncomfortably with our experience.

I was not to know where this incident would lead. Later, we would meet John Holt and have him stay with us in Birmingham while he was on a European lecture tour. Later still, Shirley and John were both to die of cancer, both in their prime, two bright lights both extinguished within a few years of each other.

The central message of *How Children Fail* was stark: *most children fail in school, and indeed, given the model on which we set up schools, could hardly do anything else*. Most fail in the school- and society-defined tasks of first learning the imposed curriculum and then passing the tests derived from it. That was a grim verdict in itself, although not a new one. A former chief inspector of schools for England and Wales, Edmond Holmes, had come to similar conclusions about the first National Curriculum, which he had spent thirty years trying to implement. His two books, *What Is and What Might Be* (1911) and *The Tragedy of Education* (1913, revised 1921), described the results of such an approach. John Holt went further and pointed to a deeper sense of failure:

> They fail to develop more than a tiny part of the tremendous capacity for learning, understanding, and creating with which they were born and of which they made full use during the first two or three years of their lives. (*How Children Fail*, p. 9)

Holt proposed that school, in collusion with the dominant parts of the culture in which it operated, actually *reduced* the intelligence of most children, so that they came out after 15,000 hours or so of schooling less intelligent than when they went in. In *How Children Fail*, Holt was concerned to show how he had come to this conclusion. More importantly, in his observations in classrooms he attempted to uncover the underlying mechanisms or, in the current educational newspeak, the nature of 'the delivery systems'.

How to make schools worse

There is a terrible irony in rereading John Holt's message. Most of the bad strategies he identified that were fostered in the private schools, in which he taught, and made his observations and analysis, are those which raise children's fears and produce learning that is fragmented, distorted and short-lived. They have become the basic building blocks of the second National Curriculum for England and Wales as well as the US schooling system. Indeed, most schooling systems throughout the world show the same basic characteristics, as Clive Harber points out in his *Schooling as Violence* (2004), a survey of the consequences of schooling across the world. Consequently, school has been made even worse. The same process was evident in the last few years of Holt's life in the USA, and he contemplated writing a book entitled *How to Make Schools Worse* to document the regressive developments as they occurred. As has already been mentioned, he founded the organization *Growing Without Schooling* instead, of which more in a later chapter.

He also demonstrated the failure of the ideas of the 'progressives' about making school work better:

They thought, or at least talked and wrote as if they thought, that there were good and bad ways to coerce children (the bad ones mean, harsh, cruel, the good ones gentle, persuasive, subtle, kindly), and that if they avoided the bad and stuck to the good they would do no harm. (*How Children Fail*, p. 175)

As an example, he looked at the 'New Mathematics' and was unimpressed. What he saw was the old mathematics rearranged in a different pattern. It was still cookbook mathematics even if some of the recipes looked newer and more inviting. Holt proposed that children cannot learn much of any use from 'cookbooks', new or old, because they learn effectively not by trying to transplant someone else's reality into their own but by building up their own reality from the experiences they encounter. This was how young children learned and why they were such prolific and successful learners, a theme Holt took up in his last book, *Learning All the Time*.

A second irony is that Holt has been labeled as a 'progressive' himself and identified with the very ideas he sought to expose. There was, he maintained, no way to coerce children without making them afraid, or more afraid. Fear is the inescapable companion of coercion and its inescapable consequence. Progressive education merely tried to find a kindly way to coerce children; the learning remained teacher directed in a place of required attendance. Holt proposed that we must reject, therefore, the idea of schools and classrooms as places where, most of the time, children are doing what adults tell them to do, if we are serious about *educating* them rather than *schooling* them.

The questions Holt set out to answer were these: How does this mass failure take place? What really goes on in the classroom? What are these children who fail, doing? What goes on in their heads? Why don't they make more use of their capacity?

His thinking began as a series of memos written in the evenings to a colleague and friend whose fifth-grade class he both observed and taught during the day. Later he arranged these memos under four main headings that reflected the themes that had emerged during his observations: 'Strategy', 'Fear and Failure', 'Real Learning' and 'How Schools Fail'.

Holt taught in private schools with reputations for high standards and he was at pains to point out that his book was not about 'bad' schools or 'backward' children – indeed, almost the reverse. Parents were paying out good money to have their children attend these schools. To all outward appearances the schools and the children were 'successful'. The harmful effects of the schooling in question were ignored, not least because they were somewhat subtle in their operation:

Strategy deals with the ways in which children try to meet, or dodge, the demands that adults make on them in school. *Fear and Failure* deals with the interaction in children of fear and failure and the effect of this on strategy and learning. *Real Learning* deals with the difference between what the children appear to know or are expected to know, and what they really know. *How Schools Fail* analyses the ways in which schools foster bad strategies, raise children's fears, produce learning which is usually fragmented, distorted and short-lived, and generally fail to meet the real needs of children. (*How Children Fail*, p. 10)

Strategies in classrooms

There were various strategies that emerged from Holt's observations. Some children resist any involvement at all because they do not want the embarrassment of making mistakes, and learn to avoid it. Others attempt to find tricks to locate the right answer. They are the 'producers' who focus on feeding their teachers the right answers that, they signal, they so clearly prize above all else. 'Producers' jump at right answers, and if they fail to give them, they fall back into despair or defeat. The harm is even greater if they do get right answers by their strategies:

> When a child gets right answers by illegitimate means, and gets credit for knowing what he doesn't know, it does double harm. First, he doesn't learn, his confusions are not cleared up; secondly, he comes to believe that a combination of bluffing, guessing, mind reading, snatching at clues, and getting answers from other people is what he is supposed to do at school; that this is what school is all about; that nothing else is possible. (*How Children Fail*, p. 146)

Others try to please the teacher, whether they have any clue as to the right answer or not, by waving their hands in the air enthusiastically – provided at least six others, including some successful 'producers', have their hands in the air too. A common strategy, Holt noted, was mumbling answers, for a teacher anxious to get a right answer will assume that anything that sounds close is meant to be the right answer. An associated strategy is 'guess and look':

> There was a good deal of the tried-and-true strategy of *guess-and-look*, in which you start to say a word, all the while scrutinizing the teacher's face to see whether you are on the right track or not. With most teachers no further strategies are needed. (*How Children Fail*, p. 29)

A few children are 'thinkers' who try to assess meaning and work for understanding despite the dominance of the 'right answer' culture. They are not helped by teachers who have such a fixed idea of the answer they require that they dismiss answers offered which are logical, or even alternative correct answers. The culture of right answerism has another unhelpful tendency, which is to value the 'yes' and other positive answers more than the 'no' and negative ones even when the information yielded was the same:

> This, of course, is the result of their miseducation, in which 'right answers' are the only ones that pay off. They have not learned how to learn from a mistake, or even that learning from mistakes is possible. If they say, 'Is the number between 5,000 and 10,000?' and I say yes, they cheer; if I say no, they groan, even though they get exactly the same amount of information in either case. (*How Children Fail*, p. 46)

Relief often follows a mistake, for correct answers create a strain and anxiety because more right answers are then expected. The consequence is a low tolerance of uncertainty in both teachers and taught, because answer grabbing and teacher pleasing take continual precedence over thinking and understanding.

Holt concludes that the results of all this are far from trivial. The strategies are defensive in attempting to avoid trouble, disapproval, loss of status, embarrassment, ridicule and other punishment. They are fear-laden and neurotic. They are self-limiting and self-defeating. In the process, children's intelligence is destroyed and their behavior becomes more and more stress laden. They are learning to behave stupidly in the school's terms in its 'temple of right answerism', with the 'teacher high priests' devoted to the doctrine of 'tell them and test them'. Only the few determined 'thinkers' can ride out this system and survive intact.

Teacher versus pupil interpretations of intelligent behavior in schools

But from the children's point of view, their behavior is intelligent because it minimizes stress. They give up on thinking school will ever make much sense. The point is to survive each day with as much dignity intact as possible: 'For children the central business of school is not learning, whatever this vague word means, it is getting these daily tasks done, or at least out of the way, with a minimum of effort and unpleasantness' (*How Children Fail*, p. 37). But this approach neither serves them well in the pursuit of the school's desires nor develops their confidence as learners with understanding.

Furthermore, it does not match the teacher's idea of taking the students on a journey to some glorious destination well worth the pains of the trip:

> So the valiant and resolute band of travellers I thought I was leading towards a much-hoped-for destination turned out instead to be much more like convicts in a chain gang, forced under threat of punishment to move along a rough path leading nobody knew where, and down which they could hardly see more than a few steps ahead. School feels like this to children: it is a place where *they* make you go and where *they* tell you to do things and where *they* try to make your life unpleasant if you don't do them or don't do them right. (*How Children Fail*, p. 37)

Tests just make things worse

These false messages about learning are reinforced by tests. Tests are supposed to make children work harder. Holt disagreed. Since children tend to feel threatened by tests, they work worse, not better. Scared soldiers might be thought to fight better, but a scared learner is almost always a poor learner.

Tests are supposed to show what children have learned. But teachers everywhere need good test results as much as, if not even more than, children, to prove that they are 'good' teachers. So tests are announced in advance and the type of contents outlined. Practicing and coaching in the kind of material to appear in the tests then follows. Students recognize the dishonesty of stressing and rewarding this shallow appearance of knowledge rather than working for real, deep understanding:

> In short, our 'Tell-'em and test-'em' way of teaching leaves most students increasingly confused, aware that their academic success rests on shaky foundations, and convinced that school is mainly a place where you follow meaningless procedures to get meaningless answers to meaningless questions. (*How Children Fail*, p. 151)

Why children fail

From his observations, John Holt provided three answers to the question of why children fail. They fail because they are afraid, or bored, or confused. These often occur in combination. They are afraid, above all else, of failing, of disappointing or displeasing the many anxious adults around them 'whose limitless hopes and expectations for them hang over their heads like a cloud' (*How Children Fail*, p. 10).

They are bored because most of the things they are given and told to do in school are so trivial and dull. They make such limited and narrow demands on the wide spectrum of their intelligence, capabilities and talents.

They are confused because most of the torrent of words that pours over them in school makes little or no sense. It often flatly contradicts other things they have been told, and hardly ever has any relation to what they already know – to the rough model of reality that they carry around in their heads.

Chapter 4

How Children Learn

People sometimes express disappointment on reading John Holt's second book, *How Children Learn*, after the provocative nature of the first. Part of the reason may be the switch from the challenging emphasis of the first book to the steadier and slower task of beginning some reconstruction work in schools, which at this point in his thinking he believed might be possible.

In *How Children Fail*, Holt described children using their minds badly. They are induced by the standard school regime to use their minds not to learn but to get out of doing the things imposed on them by adults. In the short run, these strategies work and make it possible for children to get through their schooling even though they learn very little of use in the process. In the long term, the result is far from trivial: it is the destruction of effective intelligence so that children are prevented from growing into more than limited versions of the confident, courageous and effective learners they might have become.

In *How Children Learn*, the task Holt set himself was to explore those situations in which children use their minds well, learning boldly and effectively. Most of the examples to be found were of children learning before starting school:

> In short, children have a style of learning that fits their condition, and which they use naturally and well until we train them out of it. We like to say that we send children to school to teach them to think. What we do, all too often, is to teach them to think badly, to give up a natural and powerful way of thinking in favour of a method that does not work well for them and that we rarely use ourselves. (*How Children Learn*, p. 7)

Perhaps a different vision of school was possible, and if we had a better understanding of how children learn, we might be able to reconstruct schools so that they became places where all children grew not just in size but in curiosity, confidence, courage, independence, resourcefulness, resilience, patience and competence.

Some features of effective learning were already known but largely ignored, Holt pointed out. First, we know that vivid, vital, pleasurable experiences are the easiest to remember. Second, we know that memory works best when unforced, and that 'it is not a mule that can be made to walk by beating it'. We also know that we think badly, and even perceive badly, when we are afraid, anxious or under stress. These are the situations in which we say 'we are just not thinking straight at the moment'. In Holt's view this describes the emotional atmosphere of most classrooms most of the time.

These two enterprises of understanding better how children learn, and then reconstructing schools in the light of these understandings, might take some time, Holt thought, and we may find, in 50 or 100 years, that all of what we think of as our most up-to-date notions about school, teaching and learning are either completely inadequate or just mistaken.

These tasks also require the exercise of caution – what Bertrand Russell called constructive doubt and others have seen as the skeptical approach:

> There's an old story about two men on a train. One of them, seeing some naked-looking sheep in a field, said, 'those sheep have just been sheared'. The other looked a moment longer, and then said, 'they seem to be – on this side'. It is in such a cautious spirit that we should say whatever we have to say about the workings of the mind, and it is in this spirit that I have tried to write, and in which I hope others will read, this book. (*How Children Learn*, p. 9)

The book is divided into five main parts followed by a concluding chapter. The five parts are 'Games and Experiments', 'Talk', 'Reading', 'Sports', and 'Art, Maths and Other Things'. Each section contains observations of children in learning situations and Holt's interpretations of the events. His intention, Holt states, is to locate and describe effective learning more than to explain it.

Lisa, aged 16 months, is the subject of several of the observations in the part entitled 'Games and Experiments'. Her work, which adults might call play, is accompanied by pseudo-speech she has invented. She fits screws and other small objects neatly into their holes, and this makes Holt wonder if the clumsiness of small children is overstated. Holt's typewriter provides other opportunities for investigation, and her actions with the machine become more refined and controlled by both practice and imitation. The piecing together of cause and effect is a constant part of Lisa's work:

> This morning Lisa bent down to pick up a balloon and, as she did, a puff of wind coming through the door blew the balloon across the floor. She watched it go. When it stopped, she moved close to it, and blew at it, as if

to make it go further. This surprised me. Can such young children make a connection between the ability of the wind to move objects, and their own ability to move them by blowing on them? Apparently they can. (*How Children Learn*, p. 15)

Because we tend to underestimate children, we can easily overlook the nature of what they are doing. Lisa walks round the balloon singing but she changes her song and then changes it again until it is a different song altogether. A musician might call it variations on a theme. Singing is usually encouraged in the first encounters with school, Holt notes, but they all sing the same songs taught by the teacher, who often aims to 'get them right', not to make up something new. Uniformity takes over from improvisation.

Small children are self-motivated, Holt observes, but school sets about substituting external motivation and then worrying about why this is so ineffective:

It is not hard to feel that there must be something very wrong with much of what we do in school, if we feel the need to worry so much about what many people call 'motivation'. A child has no stronger desire than to make sense of the world, to move freely in it, to do the things he sees the bigger people doing. (*How Children Learn*, p. 17)

He muses that good presents for young children might be eggbeaters, flash-lights or saucepans. If they get broken, it costs little. Later, thousands of pounds will be spent on trying to get children learning, so begrudging the cost of a few household objects is a false economy.

From his observations, Holt proposes that games are a prolific source of learning. Spontaneous games often begin by accident. The spirit behind them is sometimes joy, sometimes foolishness, at other times exuberance, but they all involve finding out how the world works. So, education might be regarded as a huge game, 'the game of trying to find out how the world works':

Recently Lisa has started to play fierce games. She bares her teeth, growls, roars, rushes at me. I pretend to be afraid, and cower behind a chair. It can go on for some time. From this, and many other things she does, it seems as if she feels a Me inside her growing stronger, doing things, demanding things. Any game that makes Me seem more powerful must be a good game. Most of the time she knows all too well how powerless that Me is ... Children don't mind letting us the adults win the game, as long as we let them score a few points. But so many of us, like some football coaches, seem never to be content with merely winning; we have to run up the big score. (*How Children Learn*, pp. 20–1)

Throughout the book, John Holt's stories about children learning are used to reflect and draw out some ideas about effective learning. From observing Lisa he notes a series of points. She does not feel she has to get everything right before starting but is willing to begin by doing something and then modifying it. Next, she is not satisfied with incorrect imitations but keeps looking and comparing until she is satisfied she has got it correct.

Lisa copes well with uncertainty. She hears things all day that currently make no sense to her, but she doesn't appear to mind: 'She lives in uncertainty as naturally and easily as a fish lives in water' (*How Children Learn*, p. 23). When do children begin to crave certainty?

How do they catch fear of uncertainty, and many other fears, from others? Holt noted that Lisa never seemed to be afraid of bugs, but after she witnessed someone else screaming because of the presence of a spider, she became wary, drew away from all insects and spiders, and did not want to watch them. Part of her curiosity about the world had been killed off.

Yet, when Lisa was interested in something, her patience and concentration could be astonishing. Her learning was an end in itself and she was not doing it to please an adult or gain someone's approval. A mother wrote to John Holt and seemed to throw some light on this. She said of her son that he hated to be taught but loved to learn things. Is learning in order to please adults and submission to unwanted teaching something that will be caught later in the competitive and status-conscious situations of a nursery school?

Holt concludes this part of the book by commenting on the *apparent* inefficiency of children's learning. They often pile up a lot of raw sensory data before trying to sort those data and make sense of them. Until this has happened, they may have no clear ideas about what questions they are going to start asking. Adults would usually move much more quickly into imposing a pattern, almost any pattern, to cope with their inability to tolerate confusion and uncertainty. But the child's method is superior in situations that are new and confusing. Moreover, real-life situations are typically new and confusing, and the child's method prevents them from coming to hasty and erroneous conclusions on the basis of too little evidence. Most schooling discourages this approach, which is then doomed to become stunted and subsequently destroyed.

Next, Holt proposes that the most difficult thing we ever learn is to talk. It takes very subtle and complicated coordination of lips, tongue, teeth, palate, jaws, cheeks, voice and breath. So, how is it learned? The answer appears to be by patient and persistent experiment, by carefully comparing the results of these experiments with the speech of the other people around, and by not being afraid to get things wrong before setting about correcting them.

There is a contrast between this natural, effective method of learning and the stilted, ineffective methods schools usually seek to put in its place. The remark that if we tried to 'teach' children to talk, they would never learn it, is used to speculate how a committee of experts would set about devising a talking curriculum. There would be lists of speech skills, words, syllables and sounds. There would be plenty of drill, review and tests. Holt forecasts that most children would become baffled, discouraged, humiliated and fearful and would give up trying to learn to talk.

Lisa grew up on a cattle ranch and so it was no surprise that at 18 months she was pointing at cattle and saying, 'See cows, see cows.' A few days later she said the same thing to a field with some horses in it and later to a field of sheep. We did not correct her. She had apparently isolated a class that we would call 'large animals in fields' and had identified them as cows. By listening to others talking she realized that there were subgroups to her classification and learned to put the conventional name on each one. The adults around were allowing her powers of self-correction to operate and her confidence in being able to work it out:

> A child's understanding of the world is uncertain and tentative. If we question him too much or too sharply, we are more likely to weaken that understanding than strengthen it. His understanding will grow faster if we can make ourselves have faith in it and leave it alone. (*How Children Learn*, p. 65)

In any case, classifying is a matter not just of sorting words but of complex understandings such as that a similarity is a difference that does not make any difference. Thus, although chairs may differ in details, they are all essentially the same. 'Telling the answer' looks like a helpful thing to do and sometimes it is, especially when asked a question, but letting children work it out encourages their thinking strategies.

The adult anxiety to get it right immediately can be counterproductive. Holt cites Patrick, who at two years of age could not pronounce S, Z, SH, CH, or any other similar sounds. 'Spoon' came out as 'poon'. Nobody fretted, and before long he had put the matter right by himself. But supposing the adults had been correcting him every time he spoke? He might have just got discouraged and reticent, or he could have developed a stutter or a stammer, since research has shown this is at least one way that stutters develop.

This approach always upsets some people. After meetings where John Holt was speaking, he often received letters challenging him on this point. One psychologist asserted that we should correct all the mistakes that children made. Holt wrote explaining further how counterproductive this can be, but to no avail. Evidence was not the issue, he concluded, but belief in the indispensability of experts. Anyone who makes it their life's work to help others can fall into the trap of believing that the 'clients' cannot really get along without them and reject any evidence that they are frequently capable of standing on their own feet. 'Many people seem to have built their lives around the notion that they are in some way indispensable to children, and to question this is to attack the very centre of their being' (*How Children Learn*, p. 69).

Children who start to talk, however, are taking a bold leap into the world. Anyone who has tried to use a foreign language in another country experiences the same thing. You are encouraged if the native speaker tolerates your halting attempts to use the unfamiliar words, but discouraged if you encounter one who insists on 'teaching' you the correct grammar and the perfect pronunciation. Holt recounts his own experiences in trying to speak Italian when he spent a year in Italy, where he encountered many helpful and patient Italians:

A child learning to talk needs the kind of curious, attentive, sympathetic audience that I found in Italy. At first, he is not sure that this language business really works. Even after many years of talking, he may not feel that he can get his most important thought and feelings across to other people. (*How Children Learn*, p. 71)

In Italy, this tact is extended to children, but this is not necessarily so elsewhere. It seems, Holt observes, to be a rule in the USA and the UK that you should be tactful with other adults and not insistently point out their speech errors, but this courtesy is not automatically extended to children. It is no surprise, therefore, that children do not particularly like to hear stories about their younger days. What seems cute to adults is a reminder to children of their smallness, helplessness and clumsiness. Childhood is not a blessed, romantic state of bliss, but a state of powerlessness and something to escape from as quickly as possible and then to be largely forgotten. This became the theme of Holt's later, radical book *Escape from Childhood*.

Classrooms do not necessarily help children become better at talking. Lack of conversation is likely to lead to poor readers and poor writers later:

Bill Hull once said to me, 'Who needs the most practice talking in school? Who gets the most?' Exactly. The children need it, the teacher gets it ... The result of this kind of education is that children of ten or even older may be no better at talking than they were at five. (*How Children Learn*, p. 76)

Holt did not see 'progressive' ideas as much of an improvement. He did not see the so-called revolution of the 1960s as altering things much, since the stilted question-and-answer sessions and the brief fake discussion and conversation interludes were little or no improvement on telling and lecturing. No real increased practice in talking took place.

The next theme explored is that of reading. Many of the observations made about talk are now applied here. Again, the stress is on giving children support while they learn to figure things out and avoiding actions that emphasize their limited competence.

Holt notes that children often learn well from slightly older children. One reason may be that the older child understands the language of the younger and can speak in their terms. But another is that the gap in competence is not so forbidding; the older child is more within reach than the adults. Adults who can read well can easily forget the problems of decoding print. One way to remind ourselves is to try to make sense of an unfamiliar script:

> One day I took a sheet of printing in some Indian language, and tried to find the words that occurred most often on the page. It was amazingly difficult. At first the page looked like nothing but a jumble of strange shapes. Even when I was concentrating on one short, common word, it took a long time before I could recognize that word at sight and pick it out of the others. Often I would go right by without noticing it. (*How Children Learn*, p. 91)

In the same way, he concludes, it takes children time to get used to the shapes of letters, and if they come from homes where reading is less prevalent, they will need to go through this familiarization stage in the classroom. Again, the self-checking and self-correcting skills should be allowed to operate, and rushing in to correct mistakes too soon or too often only serves to extinguish these skills. 'What we must remember about this ability of children to become aware of mistakes, to find and correct them, is that it takes time to work, and that under pressure and anxiety, it does not work at all' (*How Children Learn*, p. 94).

One source of pressure is the timetable. Holt expresses his exasperation with this kind of thinking about learning:

> Timetables! We act as if children were railroad trains running on a schedule. The railroad man figures that if his train is going to get to Chicago at a certain time, then it must arrive on time at every stop along the route. If it is ten minutes late getting into a station, he begins to worry. In the same way, we say that if children are going to know so much when they go to college, then they have to know this at the end of this grade, and

that at the end of that grade. If the child does not arrive at one of these intermediate stations when we think he should, we instantly assume that he is going to be late at the finish. But children are not railroad trains. They don't learn at an even rate. They learn in spurts, and the more interested they are in learning, the faster these spurts are likely to be. (*How Children Learn*, p. 100)

The next theme is that of learning and sports. Most of the observations are drawn from young children learning to swim. He notes the developing interest and confidence of the infant Tommy as he is taken regularly to the pool. His progress in exploring was uneven. His courage to try new things rose and fell like the tide. The baby in the pool had moments of courage and exploration and then times of retreat and retrenchment. Tommy sometimes let John tow him around in the water, kicking his feet and paddling with his hands, but then he would revert to wanting to hold on to him tight or be held tight.

Other parents would try to teach their infants to swim without getting very far because they were not sensitive enough to this rise and fall of courage. They could end up with a counterproductive experience. One parent succeeded in reducing all three of his children to tears and terror in this way:

If we continually try to force a child to do what he is afraid to do, he will become more timid, and will use his brains and energy, not to explore the unknown, but to find ways to avoid the pressure we put on him. (*How Children Learn*, p. 111)

Holt next turns his attention to art, maths and 'other things', and invokes the research of David Hawkins on learning science. Hawkins found that when he made it a rule that children have a period of completely free play with the materials before going on to any directed work, the quality of the learning increased. Hawkins proposed that we have to cross the line between ignorance and insight several times before we truly understand, and that dragging or shoving us across does not do all that much good. A theme that Holt develops in his later books begins here, that teachers may teach but that learning does not necessarily follow: 'We teachers like to think that we can transplant our own mental models into the minds of children by means of explanations. It can't be done' (*How Children Learn*, p. 143). From his careful observations of children, John Holt sees it differently. Children see the world as a whole, even if it is a mysterious whole. They make their own paths into the unknown, often using routes we may not have anticipated. When they learn this way, following their curiosity, children go faster and cover more territory.

Finally, there is a section entitled 'The Mind at Work', where the strands of the earlier observations are pulled together. Holt reflects on how children seemed better able to solve a commercial puzzle than he could, and decides it was because he tried to reason about the puzzle far too soon, whereas children explored the pieces thoroughly and experimented with them randomly. With this thorough awareness of what the pieces were like and what they could do, they could then start to apply reason to the solution. This was not an attack on the value of analytical, deductive, logical reasoning. Detectives, scientists and car mechanics make great use of it. But it needs to be kept in its appropriate place, and it is less useful in education than we are led to believe. Teachers are encouraged to accept an 'astonishing delusion'. They are pressed to believe in the magic power of explanation:

> We think we can take a picture, a structure, a working model of something, constructed in our minds out of long experience and familiarity, and by turning that model into a string of words, transplant it whole into the mind of someone else. (*How Children Learn*, p. 164)

Although this sometimes works, it does not do so very often, and most of the time explaining does not increase understanding all that much, and may even lessen it. Holt recognizes that this conclusion makes defenders of the system angry. They say we have to teach the children symbols because human knowledge is stored that way. They do not recognize that teaching the symbols – that is, explaining them in words – does not produce any more than shallow understanding at best:

> They have to make the journey from reality to symbol many times, before they are ready to go the other way ... But when we do what we do most of the time in school – beginning with meaningless symbols and statements, and trying to fill them with meaning by way of explanations, we only convince most children either that all symbols are meaningless or that they are too stupid to get meaning from them. (*How Children Learn*, p. 166)

The natural learning style of children impresses John Holt. Because they are curious and want to make sense out of the world, and to gain competence and control over themselves and their surroundings, they are experimental, open, receptive and perceptive. They do not sit back and observe the world, but taste it, feel it, touch it, push and pull it, and generally explore it. They are bold – in spasms – and not afraid to make mistakes and learn from them. They do not have to have instant meaning but can be patient while meaning emerges.

In contrast, school is a place that initially supports this style, but then gives less and less time, opportunity or reward for this kind of thinking and learning. Instead, it sets about gradually undermining confidence in this approach and replacing it with something far less effective, which is ultimately counterproductive by turning most children off learning altogether. Holt states his hope that we *can* devise schools that get back to the effectiveness of natural learning:

> What is essential to realize is that children learn independently, not in bunches; that they learn out of interest and curiosity, not to please or appease the adults in power; and that they ought to be in control of their own learning, deciding for themselves what they want to learn and how they want to learn it. (*How Children Learn*, p. 169)

Two objections are commonly raised against this proposal. The first is that this implies that children have to reinvent the whole culture for themselves. It is the word 'discover' that creates the problem here. The whole culture is out there already invented, but the method of learning about it that is being proposed is firsthand and not the prevalent thirdhand approach of accepting the secondhand verbal accounts of others.

The second is the 'essential knowledge' belief. Holt sees this idea as full of fallacies. People cannot agree what this essential knowledge consists of. Therefore, it is no surprise to find that the various national curriculum offerings around the world differ astonishingly in their contents.

Next, there appears to be no knowledge that is essential for everyone that they will not encounter anyway. This was how they absorbed the essential bits of knowledge needed to master the skills of talking.

Furthermore, knowledge changes so rapidly that what is seen as essential one year simply becomes fallacious or redundant later. Believers in essential knowledge decreed that when Holt was in school he should study physics and chemistry. Of his chemistry, he could remember only two or three formulae and a concept called 'valence'. He mentioned valence to a chemist one day, who laughed:

> When I asked what was so funny, he said, 'Nobody talks about valence any more; it's an outmoded concept'. But the rate of discovery being what it is, the likelihood that what children learn today will be out of date in twenty years is much *greater* than it was when I was a student. (*How Children Learn*, pp. 170–1)

Observing young children learning leads John Holt to propose that they are natural learners, that birds fly, fish swim, and humans learn and think. Therefore, we do not need to 'motivate' children into learning, by wheedling, bribing or bullying them. We do not need to keep picking away at their minds to make sure they are learning:

> What we need to do, and all we need to do, is bring as much of the world [as possible] into the school and the classroom; give children as much help and guidance as they need and ask for; listen respectfully when they feel like talking; and then get out of the way. We can trust them to do the rest. (*How Children Learn*, p. 172)

Chapter 5

The Underachieving School

John Holt's third book was a miscellany of 16 short pieces, many of which had appeared as articles in pamphlets, magazines or books. Acknowledgments are given to *Harper's Magazine, Life, The New York Review of Books, The New York Times Magazine*, the *PTA Magazine, Redbook* and *Yale Alumni Magazine*. In the foreword, Holt noted that his thinking about education was undergoing radical change and that the essays reflect this. These pieces form a list of questions and doubts that Holt felt he had to investigate.

In 'True Learning' he began to signal his growing unease about schooling. His starting point was that education is not what someone gives or does to someone else, but something people do for themselves. He pointed to a mismatch between the learner's needs and the school experience that is imposed:

> What young people need and want to get from their education is: one, a greater understanding of the world around them; two, a greater development of themselves; three, a chance to find their work, that is, a way in which they may use their own unique tastes and talents to grapple with the real problems of the world around them and to serve the cause of humanity. (*The Underachieving School*, p. 13)

Society also requires three things: first, that the traditions and higher values of the culture be passed on, along with, second, a general acquaintance of the world in which we are living; and third, some preparation for employment. All these tasks used to be undertaken by the family in the community until mass schooling was adopted. Schools, however, are proving to be inadequate for the task:

> None of them is done well by schools. None of them can or ought to be done by the schools solely or exclusively. One reason the schools are in trouble is that they have been given too many functions that are not properly or exclusively theirs. (*The Underachieving School*, p. 13)

Schools therefore should be a resource from which people can take what they need in the activity of educating themselves. Given that there are many roads to education, each learner should be free to find and devise his or her own route.

A short essay, 'A Little Learning', dealt with some reservations he had about Piaget's theory of learning and the nature of the experiments on which it was based. These relied too much on the idea that thinking in its highest form is mostly the manipulation of verbal symbols. But when children give 'wrong' answers, it may often be that they are answering a different question. For example, when Piaget asks a young child whether two rods are the same length when the ends are lined up, they agree. But when one has been moved so that the ends are no longer in line, they say one is longer. But they may be answering a different question about whether one is now sticking out past the other. The question 'which is longer?' can have more than one meaning.

In 'Schools Are Bad Places for Kids', Holt began by noting that there was a desire, among many people he had talked with, to make schools better places, but they either did not know how to do so or do not dare to do it. The children are mostly helpless, for they do not know what is being done to them and, even if they work it out, they are told it is being done to them by kindly-intentioned people and for their own good.

For the most part, children arrive at school as curious, patient, energetic and skillful learners who have already directed their own learning of their mother tongue and encouraged the adults around them to perform as learning coaches in this endeavor. Gradually, this confidence is broken down by a series of messages, the first of which is that you come to school to learn. But, Holt protests, they were learning before, and very effectively too.

The message that is gradually introduced is that children cannot really be trusted to learn and are no good at it, so adults need to control and direct their learning. The *best* of early childhood education, of course, does no such thing, but encourages the development of the natural learning skills children bring to school with them. But this is only a delaying experience and the other messages are introduced sooner or later.

There are other messages. Personal curiosity is not encouraged. To be wrong, or uncertain, or confused, is a crime. What is required are the skills of 'practical slavery':

There is much fine talk in schools about Teaching Democratic Values. What the children really learn is Practical Slavery. How to suck up to the boss. How to keep out of trouble, and get other people in. 'Teacher, Billy is . . .' Set into mean-spirited competition against other children, he learns that every man is the natural enemy of every other man. Life, as the

strategists say, is a zero-sum game: what one wins, another must lose, for
every winner there must be a loser. (Actually, our educators, above all our
so-called and self-styled prestige universities, have turned education into a
game where for every winner there are twenty losers.) (*The Underachieving
School*, p. 25)

School becomes a long lesson in 'how to turn yourself off' – for 'Sit still! Be
quiet!' are the great watchwords of the enterprise, a behavior requirement
guaranteed to induce high levels of passivity and then stupidity. The teachers
are no more free to respond openly and honestly to the students than the
students are free to respond to the teachers or each other. Where the air
practically vibrates with suspicions and anxiety, the child learns to live in a
kind of daze, saving their energies for those parts of their life that are of
little interest to adults. The peer group moves in to fill this gap with its own
compulsory culture of music, fashion and antagonism to adults.

The remedies Holt proposed are radical:

1. Abandon or modify drastically the compulsory attendance laws.
2. Experiment with 'schools without walls' approaches.
3. Involve many more people who are not teachers in learning situations.
4. Encourage students to teach each other.
5. Let children judge their own work.
6. Abolish the fixed, required curriculum.

It comes down, Holt argued, to whether we are on the side of slavery or
freedom:

What it all boils down to is, are we trying to raise sheep – timid, docile,
easily driven or led – or free men? If what we want are sheep, our schools
are perfect as they are. If what we want is free men, we'd better start
making some big changes. (*The Underachieving School*, p. 36)

In 'The Fourth R: The Rat Race', Holt continued to display misgivings
about the whole formal educational enterprise. Although schools may claim
to be victims of society's expectations, Holt observed that this is only partly
true and that schools are also the source of miseducation: 'It is only in
theory, today, that educational institutions serve the student; in fact, the
real job of a student at any ambitious institution is, by his performance, to
enhance the reputation of that institution' (*The Underachieving School*, p. 37).

There is far more concern that the student is not doing right by the
school than that the school is not doing right by the student. Indeed, in
the latter case the blame is put firmly on the 'bad' student. In the service
of the school's reputation, children have not worked such long hours since

the early and brutal days of the Industrial Revolution. These pressures have destructive effects, for they create 'an exaggerated concern with getting right answers and avoiding mistakes; they drive them into defensive strategies of learning and behaviour that choke off their intellectual powers and make real learning all but impossible' (*The Underachieving School*, p. 39). We give students not a sense of mission and vocation, of developing as people, as experiencing the idea that 'every person is his or her own masterpiece', but rather one of subjection and slavery instead. Learning becomes debased and corrupted, for it is not for the joy and satisfaction of finding out that students study, but to get to something else.

Holt speculated about what would happen if schools stood up for education. Supposing more and more schools began saying to colleges:

> Our best students are fed up with grinding for grades: they want to learn for the interest and joy of learning. Unless you show them, and us, that you are making grades less important, they are going to look for other colleges to go to, and we are going to help them. (*How Children Learn*, p. 76)

Might this not change the picture? After all, pressure can be exerted both ways, he suggested.

In 'Teachers Talk Too Much', a familiar theme in Holt's writing is introduced briefly, of how non-stop-talking teachers turn children into bad, passive and inefficient learners. A telling image of the sheepdog is employed:

> So we have these flocks of school children, twenty-five or more of them, that we are trying to lead or drive down a chosen road. They don't all want to go down that road; maybe none of them do; maybe they have other things they would rather do or think about. So we continually have to round them up and move them along, like a sheep dog herding sheep. Only, our voice is the dog. (*The Underachieving School*, p. 47)

Next, Holt turned his attention in a longer piece to 'the tyranny of testing', in an article of that title. His proposition was that tests have no place at all in genuine education. At best, they do more harm than good; at worst, they corrupt the learning process. Tests have uses for *vocational* qualifications, for people such as surgeons, first-aiders, professional musicians or civil engineers. But testing in school is not of this type, for it has different purposes. These are, first, to coerce the inmates into doing the work; and second, to be able to hand out the rewards and penalties that all coercive systems need to exercise control over people. Holt goes on to question the belief that school testing is about quality control:

To me, it seems clear that the greater the threat posed by a test, the less it can measure, far less encourage, learning. There are many reasons for this. One of the most obvious, and most important, is that whenever a student knows he is being judged by the results of tests, he turns his attention from the material to the tester. What is paramount is not the course or its meaning to the student, but whatever is in the tester's mind. Learning becomes less a search than a battle of wits. The tester, whoever he is, is no longer a guide and helper, but an enemy. (*The Underachieving School*, p. 53)

Holt cited Howard Becker's famous study of a medical college, *Making the Grade* (New York: John Wiley, 1968), which found that 'trading for grades' and preparing for examinations replaced the learning of medicine as the main object in the behavior of students. In the task of outwitting the tester, any means seem legitimate, and cheating can become widespread.

Other objections are given. Tests almost always penalize the slower and more thorough student. They penalize anxious students who worry about tests and almost always underperform because of their mental state. Worst of all, perhaps, tests destroy self-assessment:

Perhaps the greatest of all the wrongs we do to children in school is to deprive them of the chance to judge the worth of their own work and then destroy in them the power to make such judgements, or even the belief that they can. (*The Underachieving School*, p. 56)

Holt ended the piece with a vision. What true education requires of us instead is faith and courage: faith that children want to make sense out of life and will work hard at it, courage to let them do it without continually poking, prying, prodding and meddling. 'Is this so difficult?' he asked.

The theme of 'Not So Golden Rule Days' was that compulsory school attendance stands in the way of good education. It was time for schools to get out of the jail business and into the education business instead. The two public demands that we lock up children during the daytime to keep them out of the way and then try to educate them are contradictory and self-cancelling: 'The schools can be in the jail business or in the education business, but not in both. To the extent that they are in the one they cannot be in the other' (*The Underachieving School*, p. 64). The resentment created in some inmates spills over into vandalism and the burning of schools. Teenage youths rarely throw bricks at the windows of hotels, banks or supermarkets, or set fire to them, Holt declares.

Teachers also suffer from the school attendance laws because they are diverted from educational matters into being school prison guards and school police. The primary function of teaching becomes corrupted. Coaching learners gives way to the requirement to coerce:

> The results are plain. People who go into teaching full of hope and good intentions gradually become used to thinking of themselves as policemen and of the children as their natural enemies ... It is no more possible to have open, friendly, and mutually helpful relationships between most teachers and students than it is between prison guards and prison convicts – and for exactly the same reasons. (*The Underachieving School*, p. 66)

People find it hard to believe that order will be maintained without compulsion, yet Holt observes that in the Boston Public Library he saw a great many students of all backgrounds behaving just as reasonably, sensibly and considerately as everybody else. A key difference was that they were there by choice and could leave whenever they wanted.

People protest that schools are compulsory to protect civil rights, to serve an 'entitlement' to education. In the past, this had some credibility in preventing children being used as cheap labor. But times change, and the market for child labor is hardly an issue, and, in any case, if protection is needed, it can be covered by child abuse laws. But, Holt states, compulsory schooling is now a form of child abuse and children need protection from it: 'The fact is that the only exploiters and destroyers of children today are the schools themselves' (*The Underachieving School*, p. 68).

In 'Making Children Hate Reading', John Holt addressed a regular theme in his writing: the teaching of reading, which he sees as full of harmful myths. One is the benefit of using dictionaries. Few adults learn new words this way; instead, they work out the meaning from the context. Dictionaries have only limited use in everyday living, yet they are made out to be vital when they are not. Another is the idea that you must understand everything you read. Few adults do; they select such meanings as they need and skip the rest. The way most people read magazines or newspapers gives plenty of examples of this. The result of the application of these and other myths is that learning to read is turned into a counterproductive activity:

> For most children school is a place of danger, and their main business in school is staying out of danger as much as possible. I now began to see also that books are among the most dangerous things in school. From the very beginning of school we make books and reading a constant source of possible failure and public humiliation. (*The Underachieving School*, p. 73)

The consequence is that, before long, children associate books and reading with mistakes, real or feared, and penalties and humiliations. They can easily come to the conclusion that books are best left alone as much as possible.

Holt described some of his own experiences of teaching reading. There was the day he told the class that he wanted them to read only for pleasure from now on and that he would not be checking up on their understanding of either the words or the books. The children responded, after a period of disbelief, by turning into avid readers. Using similar devices, he also freed up their writing with the 'Composition Derby', where spelling words correctly was suspended as a requirement but he offered to service their needs by writing any word they wanted on the board. He obtained furious writing activity with themes such as 'The Day the School Burned Down'. The children responded by both writing more than ever before and developing better spelling.

A shorter essay follows, entitled 'Order and Disorder'. True learning is not an orderly process to start with, Holt noted, so the idea that learning is a by-product of order is bound to be counterproductive.

In 'Teaching the Unteachable', the idea is extended to locate the kind of order being imposed and why it is rejected:

> It would be easy to compile a bookful of horror stories about schools and classrooms where neatness, mechanical accuracy, and orthodoxy of opinion – i.e. agreeing with the teacher's spoken or even unspoken notions of what is right and proper for children to believe and say – count for more than honest, independent, original expression. (*The Underachieving School*, p. 91)

A longer essay follows, entitled 'Education for the Future', and it began with what is, for John Holt, an unusually pessimistic note. He set out to write about what ought to happen, but he indicated that he did not think it likely to happen. The track record of humans is that of making more difficulties instead of resolving present ones. He was aware of the hazards of predicting the future and of the problem that single predictions lose sight of the fact that everything is interconnected and that a change in one aspect will have a knock-on effect on several others. Thus, the problems of peace, racism, work, leisure, waste, the environment, all interact with each other: 'The many problems we seem to face are in fact part of a whole problem. Unfortunately, we cannot say what the whole problem is, except by talking about the parts that make it up' (*The Underachieving School*, p. 95).

As regards education, Holt distinguished between the problems of education itself and the problems of educational institutions. The latter have an agenda of crowded classrooms, teacher shortages, buildings, finance, the impact of technology and the like. Education is concerned with the fundamental questions such as what the job of schools is and, indeed, whether they have a legitimate role at all.

In his remarks about peace, the links with education were explored. The root causes of war are to be found in the kind of people who will strive to find scapegoats on whom to focus the disappointments, envy, anger, fear and hatred they accumulate in their daily lives:

> The fundamental educational problem of our time is to find ways to help children grow into adults who have no wish to do harm. We must recognise that traditional education, far from ever solving this problem, has never tried to solve it. Indeed, its efforts have, if anything, been in exactly the opposite direction. An important aim of traditional education has always been to make children into the kind of adults who were ready to hate and kill whomever their leaders might declare to be their enemies. (*The Underachieving School*, p. 98)

Part of the reason is that education has usually been nationalistic and therefore sustaining a category of 'them', the outsiders and potential scapegoats:

> When we start talking about Them, those people on the outside, strangers, heathen, unbelievers, then the moral code goes out of the window, and everything is allowed. Lie, steal, cheat, kill, destroy, torture – nothing is too bad; in fact, the worse, the better. (*The Underachieving School*, p. 98)

This attitude spills over into policies towards the poor nations, where the problem is not so much that we lack resources but that we are short in sympathy and generosity. John Holt worked for a time in the world peace movement, so he writes here from his previous experience. Racism is another connected problem where the perceived outsiders are close at hand. It was time to think of the American Ways of Life, he felt, rather than the singular version that dominated current thinking.

The problems of work, leisure, poverty, waste and the environment, Holt saw as having a common factor in greed. Greed needs to be brought under control rather than glorified. One American responded to the idea that he could expand his business and get rich by saying that he could not eat more than four meals a day, so what was the point of getting richer? This is an attitude Holt felt should be emulated, instead of greed.

Another linking factor is lack of freedom. Most Americans are not free and have got used to being pushed around from their schooldays onwards. Greed seems like one way of becoming free: the glamorous greedy images celebrated in public life look free, but it is a false freedom based on the need to lord it over others.

Real freedom has to begin in schools that share power with children and give them freedom to move, plan and use their time, to direct and assess their own learning, and to be treated like sensible human beings:

> If we want a country in which everyone has his place, slave to everyone above him, master to everyone below him; a country in which respect for and obedience to authority is the guiding rule of life; a country, in short, like Germany in the generation before Hitler – if this is what we want, we are on the right track ...
>
> On the other hand, if we want a country in which people will resist the growing pressures to conformity and servility and will vigorously defend their own rights and the rights of others, then we had better begin to give children some real freedom in school – freedom to move, to talk, to plan and use their time, to direct and assess their own learning, to act, and be treated, like sensible human beings. (*The Underachieving School*, p. 114)

A short review of a book on teaching in an urban school is the subject of 'Blackboard Bungle'. The model proposed is based on the idea that learning is a by-product of order. This is likened to the story of the countryman's response as to how to get to the local post office. His response was that it would be best not to start from here. The model offered in the book, Holt suggests, deserves the same response, because the model is so fundamentally flawed that no amount of patching and tinkering with it will make it work. If they started with the idea that order is a by-product of real learning, things might start to change:

> Any order we get is going to have to be a by-product of real learning, learning that satisfies the curiosity of the children, that helps them to make some sense of their lives and the world they live in, that helps make these lives, if not pleasant, at least bearable. (*The Underachieving School*, p. 118)

In 'Children in Prison', teachers are the subject of scrutiny. Since new teachers are selected on the basis of their success in a system that stresses competitive examinations and the rote learning of disconnected facts, they usually carry this method forward into their own teaching. Moreover, teachers are mostly recruited from a similar background. The teachers who appeared in Boston's schools

> came from predominately non-intellectual or even anti-intellectual lower middle class backgrounds, and ... they looked on education very much as another branch of the civil service ... it was a safe, secure, and respectable way to move a rung or two from the bottom of the socio-economic ladder. (*The Underachieving School*, p. 123)

The result can too often be cohorts of dull teachers prone to overrate order, anxiously sensitive to their own authority and status, convinced that their message of 'study hard and you can be like me' has widespread appeal to the young. What could an appeal to give children more freedom possibly mean to such people, who have never been free themselves? Holt concludes that city schools fail because they are full of such teachers. In contrast, the next short piece, 'Comic Truth on an Urgent Problem', is a commentary on the work of James Herndon in a ghetto junior high school, where his success in making a few things happen in the school was seen as a threat to the system and he was ousted as a result. Dullness won the day.

The final essay is a much longer piece entitled 'Talk'. It is an account of a visit to the UK round about 1969. It begins with some comments on the role of Great Britain in the future. Although economic decline was likely to continue, with the loss of all assets of the old empire, he felt that the United Kingdom had a role in world leadership in showing that an industrialized country can be both free and civilized. As events have turned out, British governments have preferred to shame Britain's people instead with shady arms deals, a 15-year long declaration of war on Britain's own poor to further enhance the wealth of its rich people, the adoption of regressive educational policies, and a poor human rights record, having been found wanting in the eyes of the European Court many more times than any other country.

Holt then turns to education and proposes that the 'body of knowledge to be transmitted to the young' approach defies the logic of the times. He quotes the vocational educationalist from California who asked industrialists at a conference to tell him what employees were going to have to know in seven years' time. The response was hysterical laughter and the Lockheed Aircraft Corporation representative replied, 'We can't tell you what our employees need to know seven *months* from now.'

Apart from that, with knowledge increasing in quantity as well as changing in substance, we must all live with knowing only a small fraction of the knowledge at our disposal: 'We are all of us, no matter how hard we work, no matter how curious we are, condemned to grow relatively more ignorant every day we live, to know less and less of the sum of what is known' (*The Underachieving School*, p. 142). Since the experts either cannot agree or need more time to sift the evidence than events will often allow, they cannot relieve us of the responsibility to make decisions based on the best knowledge we have to hand. The consequence of this is that we have to learn to live with uncertainty and partial knowledge:

> I expect to live my entire life in uncertainty about as ignorant and uncertain and confused as I am now, and I have learned to live with this, not to worry about it. I have learned to swim in uncertainty the way a fish swims in water. (*The Underachieving School*, p. 144)

Young children are very good at this and operate with an experimental model of the world. They check, recheck and revise this model day to day and hour to hour. Only later are they introduced to the panicky quest for certainty that dominates the minds of most adults. All the things in school that contribute to this misguided quest for certainty at the expense of the confidence of children in their rather pragmatic approach are dubious. They are educationally counterproductive. Therefore:

> I don't believe in the curriculum, I don't believe in grades, I don't believe in teacher-judged learning. I believe in children learning with our assistance and encouragement the things they want to learn, when they want to learn them, how they want to learn them, why they want to learn them. This is what it seems to me education must now be about. (*The Underachieving School*, p. 146)

Such learning can take place anywhere, and it is arrogant nonsense for educators to assume or propose that any day a child does not spend in school is a day lost and wasted.

Holt goes on to answer questions put to him by members of a British audience. In answer to the observation that 'in the competition for jobs, employers are asking for tokens that children have learned an agreed, even if mostly useless, body of knowledge, and if we avoid this we are letting the children down', Holt says that public education means educating the public, and not just the public's children. We have to engage in concerted debate about any false assumptions about education that we encounter:

> The case for traditional education seems to me much weaker than it has been, and is getting ever weaker, and the case for an education which will give a child primarily not knowledge and certainty but resourcefulness, flexibility, curiosity, skill in learning, readiness to unlearn – the case ... grows ever stronger. (*The Underachieving School*, p. 155)

The next question was 'Are there still a few areas of experience through which all children should go?' Holt said he used to think this but he no longer did. He used to think mathematics was a candidate but is now dubious about its usefulness, either as a part of a preparation for life or as a tool to help intellectual growth. Mathematics, he has come to conclude, is as much entertainment as music or chess. (In passing, we can find support for Holt's view by noting that the eminent mathematician Bertrand Russell came to a similar conclusion.)

Reading, however, is different and is an essential skill, Holt says. But it still does not need to be compulsory, and most of the problems children have with reading would go away if we stopped trying to teach it to them in a formal way, but left them to learn it themselves in their own way in exactly the same way that they learned their mother tongue.

Schools based on the compulsion model perform a kind of spiritual lobotomy and are destructive of spirit, character and identity. They say to children, 'Your experience, your concern, your hopes, your fears, your desires, your interests, they count for nothing. What counts is what *we* are interested in, what *we* care about, and what *we* have decided you are to learn' (*The Underachieving School*, p. 161).

The final question put to John Holt was about teacher education. In response, he outlined his vision of effective teacher education:

> Generally speaking, I think that teachers have got to be given, in their training, the kinds of experiences we want them later to give to their children. I think they have got to be allowed to discover the pleasure and excitement of learning things for their own reasons in their own way. This coming year I am going to be teaching some education courses, one at Harvard in the fall term and a couple at the University of California in the winter term. One of the things I'm going to try to do is to put into practice what I'm talking about. I'm not going to have required assignments, tests, and grades. I'm going to give people a list of resources, and by resources I not only mean books to read but schools to visit and people to talk to and places to investigate. I'm going to say: if you want to know more about any of these things I'll tell you more, and if you want to talk about any of the things you've read or seen or investigated I'll be delighted to join you in these discussions; but *Explore!* There's what's being done, get out and look at it. (*The Underachieving School*, p. 163)

There is a postscript to the book in the form of a letter that restates many of the key points of the whole collection of essays:

1. Children learn better when they learn what they want to learn, when they want to learn it, and how they want to learn it, learning for their own curiosity and not at somebody else's order.
2. We should abolish, or largely abolish, the fixed curriculum.
3. Testing and grading corrupt and impede the learning process.
4. The act of instruction frequently impedes learning, and especially in the case of reading.
5. We should involve more people who are not teachers in learning settings.
6. We should encourage children to use the resources of the world outside the school to further their learning.
7. Compulsory school attendance no longer serves a useful educational function.

8. We should remove every possible obstacle between children and any gainful or useful contribution they want to make to society.

The title of this book, *The Underachieving School*, looks less and less secure as Holt works his way through his list of doubts. The school is not just underachieving, he seems to conclude, but acting more in keeping with Paul Goodman's proposal that school is a place of compulsory miseducation (1971).

Chapter 6

What Do I Do Monday?

What Do I Do Monday? was designed to help people to start finding their own answers to the question 'What can I do to improve learning?' by providing a few ideas that would set people, whether teachers, parents or learners, exploring the possibilities. Holt first declared his thinking to date about about learning and then went on to make some practical suggestions about beginning to change things.

At several points in the book, Holt signals how his own thinking has changed, and he starts by noting that, like many people, he used to think that learning was collecting facts or ideas. Gradually, he came to see learning as something quite different, as a kind of growing. In this, he echoes Edmond Holmes, who had come to similar conclusions in his two books *What Is and What Might Be* (1911) and *The Tragedy of Education* (1913, revised 1924), where he proposed that growing was the most appropriate simile for describing learning.

To start with, we all know much more than we can explain, using language words and many things we cannot even begin to put into words. We have grown to know what a friend looks like and are rarely fooled by lookalikes. When we taste a fruit blindfold, we know that it is a strawberry and not an apple, but cannot clearly explain how. Holt goes on to give many more examples of this kind of knowledge, the kind we have grown into through experience rather than any teaching. Our mental model is personal and extends back into our own past life. Since no two people have an identical learning biography, we can claim to have grown to be unique. Car driving provides an example of this knowledge that we have grown into by personal experience:

> The driver of a car, wanting to pass, seeing a car coming in the opposite lane, projects into the future in his mind the data he has about his car's motion and the other car's motion toward him. If it 'looks' all right, he passes. If his model is a good one, he gets by with room to spare. If his model is a bad one, he may crash. (*What Do I Do Monday?*, p. 18)

The general mental model we have developed can be seen as four worlds:

- the world inside my skin
- a second world of my personal experiences and understandings
- a third world of things that are possibilities that I know about
- and a fourth world of things as yet completely unknown.

Learning can be seen as our interaction in these four worlds. Living and learning are interactive, while learning is best seen as growing. Holt described this as the 'continuum of experience', a term he attributed to John Dewey.

School can easily become a barrier to this natural learning process and the continuum of experience. When we say to children that they come to school to learn, or to be taught how to learn, we talk nonsense:

> But the children have been learning, all the time, for all of their lives before they met us. What is more, they are very likely to be much better at learning than most of us who plan to teach them how to do it. (*What Do I Do Monday?*, p. 23)

The person who is not afraid of the world wants answers and sees life's surprises as sources of useful information. Fearful people see such surprises as attacks. They may feel invaded by new experiences. Young children learn well because they start out with the first outlook rather than the second. But in school, 'invasion' can begin, for, Holt argues, one of the things adults do, and above all in schools, is invade, in every possible way, the lives and privacy of their students. Children often become converted into fearful learners as a result, and this was the main theme of Holt's first book, *How Children Fail*: 'It seems to me a fact that the schooling of most children destroys their curiosity, confidence, trust, and therefore their intelligence' (*What Do I Do Monday?*, p. 53). Holt reported that many parents recognized this, and also that a common fear they had was that school would brutalize their children. They would say that their young children were bright, fearless, curious and lively, so they feared what would happen when they went to school. About half the people who said this, he noted, were teachers. Holt was not shy about confessing that he was part of the problem before trying to become part of the solution:

> I myself, for many or most of the years I was a teacher, did almost all of the bad things I have talked about. Indeed, I think I did most harm when my intentions were the best. Later, when I stopped trying to play God in the classroom and became more modest, I became less harmful, perhaps even useful. (*What Do I Do Monday?*, p. 53)

Another development in his thinking is reported at this point. Holt declares that he had *underestimated* the damage done by schooling in *How Children Fail*. Schooling frequently damages at a deeper level, for it destroys the health of mind and spirit of children as well. Holt is very close to the conclusions of Alice Miller in *For Your Own Good* at this point, for he notes how children are forbidden to think that their human rights are being flouted by the school:

> He is forbidden to think that these people who are doing these things to him are in any way his enemies or that they dislike or fear him. He is told to believe that they care about him, that what they do, they do for his sake, his good. He is made to feel ... he is somehow bad, wicked and really deserves harsher punishment. (*What Do I Do Monday?*, p. 55)

Holt quotes R.D. Laing and his work on madness where Laing shows that the schizoid personality does not occur through a falling apart, but a tearing apart as people are pulled apart by the activity of the people around them and the contradictory demands they make on them.

Most of our schools gradually convey to children a very powerful message that they are rather stupid, worthless, untrustworthy, unfit to make even the smallest decisions about their own lives or learning. The message is all the more powerful and effective because it is not said in words. Indeed, the teachers may well be *saying* all the time how much they like and respect children, how much they value their individual differences, how committed they are to democratic and human values, and so on. But the contradictions are lethal:

> If I tell you that you are wise, but treat you like a fool; tell you that you are good, but treat you like a dangerous criminal, you will feel what I feel much more strongly than if I said it directly. Furthermore, if I deny that there is any contradiction between what I say and what I do, and forbid you to talk or even think about such a contradiction, and say further that if you even think there may be such a contradiction it proves you are not worthy of my loving attention, my message about your badness becomes all the stronger and I am probably pushing you well along the road to craziness as well. (*What Do I Do Monday?*, p. 56)

From time to time, Holt compared the school to the army – but an army for children. Here, he notes a significant difference. The army does not *pretend* to have your welfare at heart. It does not pretend to value its soldiers as unique human beings and seek their growth, but only requires them to obey orders. It sees them merely as a means to the end of defeating the enemy and, in the end, they are expendable.

Changing things: teachers as 'travel agents'

Although teachers are restricted, they usually have more freedom of action than they think, use or believe. Teachers who do not use the opportunities will find that they are likely to shrink on the principle of 'If we don't push the walls out, they will push us in.'

Such innovative action as the situation will allow has to be used to some clear purpose, otherwise it is as foolish as asking the best route out of town without knowing where you want to go. Holt gives his destination:

> I believe we learn best when we, not others, are deciding what we are going to try to learn, and when, and how, and for what reasons or purposes; when we, not others, are in the end choosing people, materials, and experiences from which and with which we will be learning; when we, not others, are judging how easily or quickly or well we are learning, and when we have learned enough; and above all when we feel the wholeness and openness of the world around us, and our own freedom and power and competence in it. (*What Do I Do Monday?*, p. 95)

In the suggestions that follow throughout the book, Holt assumed that there is a fixed curriculum and a timetabled situation that has to be navigated. But his aim is to start a process of thinking by giving a few answers, so that people can find more answers, rather than produce a recipe book.

His first idea is to try to reduce the 'teacher as cop' pattern of behaviour and instead try to become the 'teacher as travel agent'. Those in teacher education need to do the same: to give student teachers the kind of choice and control in their learning that they may someday give in turn to their students.

The rest of the book is devoted to a few sample answers to set people working on their own answers. The first examples are in the field of numbers, arithmetic and mathematics, with the intention of exploring the continuum of human experience with numbers, starting with measuring and comparing. For example, he introduces the idea of using stopwatches in class, a novel idea in the USA at that time, and letting the children find interesting things to do with them to explore the measurement of time. Later, he goes on in other chapters to extend approaches to measuring speed, measuring strength and measuring ourselves.

Holt then turns his attention to talking and writing, and starts with the problem of bad writing:

> The bad writing from which we suffer is of two kinds. One comes from our promoters, our advertising and public relations men, our official

spokesman, our image makers, our propagandists, and worst of all, because more than anyone else they have the duty of being clear and truthful, from most of our politicians, office-holders, public servants (who think they are our masters). The other kind usually comes from our experts, our intellectuals, our academics – and sadly enough, from many of their most angry and radical critics, who too often write exactly like the professors and administrators they oppose. (*What Do I Do Monday?*, p. 173)

The first kind is bad because its motive is exploitation or manipulation, the second because language is being used to talk above the heads of most people for display and to try to establish feelings of personal superiority as experts who cannot be questioned. The result is that we feel mystified and manipulated and powerless. These feelings can then fuel the scapegoat tendency:

> All successful tyrants and dictators know that one of the most important tricks of their trade is the art of giving most people somebody they can safely push around. This was the function of the Jews in Nazi Germany. In our society, it is for many people an important function of children. (*What Do I Do Monday?*, p. 174)

Good writing makes us feel aware, informed and competent. Civilized writing of this kind starts with civilized talking and listening. Holt's suggestions range from a variety of uses for tape recorders to active lessons using interview techniques. Writing itself, 'making letters', can be demystified by investigating typography. In another chapter, Holt explores the possibilities of using cameras as a stimulus for writing and then devotes several chapters to a wealth of suggestions for developing good writing. He returns to this theme later and describes the technique of photoplay using two projectors as a means of investigating themes, and I can testify from my own experience with this method that it is a highly successful approach.

Holt then tells of his own experiments and experiences with marking and correcting work, and why he abandoned all the conventional advice on this matter because he found it to be counterproductive. First he develops a critique of marking and grading. He makes his position quite clear both to readers and to the children in his classes:

> I told the children that I did not believe in grades, that learning could not be measured and labeled with a number or letter or word, that I only gave them grades because if I didn't the school wouldn't let me teach them at all, and the grades had nothing to do with what I thought of them as people. (*What Do I Do Monday?*, p. 254)

Holt confesses that this was rather feeble and perhaps he should have fought the school on the issue even if it meant he was fired for it. Grading, he notes, is often about how quickly somebody learns something. If the aim is for children to learn long division, it is foolish to turn it into a contest to see who can learn it in the least number of tries.

Grading is also an insult to teachers and suggests that no teacher is good enough to teach all the class to succeed:

> They are saying that nobody in the college or department is a good enough teacher to be able to teach his students what he is being paid to teach them. Nobody is good enough to get all his students to do good work. (*What Do I Do Monday?*, p. 256)

Holt's advice to the teaching profession is that whatever concessions we have to make to testing, marking and grading in the short run, in the long run our duty is to oppose them, for they are anti-educational. Such a stance would begin to make teaching a real profession. To complete the process, however, would require a few more radical changes:

> Only when all parents, not just rich ones, have a truly free choice in education, when they can take their children out of a school they don't like and have a choice of many others to send them to, or the possibility of starting their own, or of educating their children outside of school altogether – only then will we teachers begin to stop being what most of us still are, and if we are honest know we are, which is jailers, baby-sitters, cops without uniforms, and begin to be professionals, freely exercising an important, valued, and honored skill and art. (*What Do I Do Monday?*, p. 265)

He was not optimistic that this would happen, not least because any move towards trying to cut down the amount of coercion, threat and punishment in schools, and to work with children on the basis of more freedom, greater respect, and helping them to manage their own learning, usually runs into problems of adjustment in the short term, in an institution that expects instant results. Children, teachers and parents will need time to adjust to a different set of principles and practices, time that is often denied.

Holt moved on to write about children in trouble, how to find ways of understanding their behavior. Most children in trouble see little reason to be any other way. Holt explains how the creative use of classrooms can be undertaken to enrich the learning environment for their sakes as well as for the sake of everyone else, and to introduce some positive reasons for changing and new activities into their lives. He is not foolish: he does not think this will be easy or automatically successful.

In the final chapter, 'Some Beginnings', there are suggestions as to how to start on the task of student-managed learning. The idea of giving over a day from time to time for a student and teacher-planned day of activities and investigations is reminiscent of the 'tenth-day initiative' adopted by Stantonbury Campus in the UK, where every tenth schoolday was eventually organized in this way. In Sweden, a proportion of the curriculum is set aside for this purpose in the legal requirements for schooling. Holt observes that in doing this kind of thinking, planning and working, the students will be getting more true learning and education than under the standard regime of the classroom.

John Holt ends with a few words about how he gave up teaching to organize a group of associates operating out of his office in Boston and elsewhere to develop ways of changing schools for the better:

> We plan to make ourselves available for short periods of time or long ones – anything from a single meeting or day of meetings to several weeks – to groups of people, whether parents, teachers, schools, school systems, or any combination of these, who want our help in making these educational changes. We will do a variety of things, speak at meetings large or small, show slides or films, visit classes and work with teachers, hold seminars or workshops, demonstrate the use of certain materials, advise on other materials, and in general be useful in whatever way we can. (*What Do I Do Monday?*, p. 310)

In response to the people who said that it was all right for a famous author like John Holt to talk like this, he replied that he had not been known at all when he began to reconstruct his thinking about education; he had been a fifth-grade teacher who had just been fired from his job and did not know where his next work was coming from. The cause is more important than such reticence:

> Every day's headlines show more clearly that the old ways, the 'tried and true' ways, are simply and spectacularly not working. No point in arguing about who's to blame. The time has come to do something very different. The way to begin is – to begin. (*What Do I Do Monday?*, p. 303)

Chapter 7

Freedom and Beyond

John Holt began *Freedom and Beyond*, published in 1972, by restating his position on learning and children. First, children are by nature smart, energetic, curious, eager to learn and good at learning, and this is clear to anyone who observes infants. Moreover, they do not need to be bribed and bullied to learn. Next, they learn best when they are happy, active, involved, and interested in what they are doing. Finally, they learn least, or not at all, when they are bored, threatened, humiliated or frightened.

Although many people admit that these four propositions are sound, it does not lead them to want to reform schools, let alone recycle them into more intelligent and dignified arrangements for learning. It concerned Holt that so many people seem to be saying that our schools must stay the way they are, or at any rate are going to stay the way they are, even if it means that children will learn less in them, or very little of any value. Therefore, our schools are the way they are for many reasons that have nothing whatever to do with children's learning. If so, 'convincing people that most of our present schools are bad for learning is not going to do much to change them; learning is not principally what they are for' (*Freedom and Beyond*, p. 2).

At this point, Holt shares his disillusion with us. He is forced to conclude that few people actually believe in freedom, although they like it as a slogan. The reason is that few people have experienced freedom and therefore cannot imagine what it is like, and easily confuse it with license. Therefore, the corporate–military model seems to be the only one people know and understand. Most people, even in democracies, tend to see democracy as a complicated process for choosing bosses to run the country, bosses whom all must then obey, with this very small difference: that every so often we get a chance to pick a new set of bosses. For the most part, people are reconciled to obedience and a modern form of slavery. Indeed, the book opens with two quotations that convey Holt's points:

Fear the man who feels himself a slave. He'll want to make a slave of you.

And:

> Obedience is the great multiplier of evil.

The dream that John Holt previously had, that schools could be places where virtue is preserved and passed on in a world otherwise empty of it, he now sees as a sad and dangerous illusion: 'The "beyond" in the title of this book means, therefore, that we must look beyond the question of reforming schools and at the larger question of schools and schooling itself' (*Freedom and Beyond*, p. 5).

Freedom in learning is obscured by a false notion of structure. The words 'structured' and 'unstructured' mislead and obscure. Almost everyone who talks or writes about learning situations that are open, free, non-coercive and learner directed calls these situations 'unstructured'. People who support open learning use these words in this way as much as people who oppose it. It is a serious error because there are no such things as 'unstructured' situations. They are not possible. Every human situation, however flexible, casual and unforced, has a structure. Instead we should speak of *different kinds of structure*, and see how they differ. One kind of structure is the traditional classroom. It is very simple. There are only two components in it. One is the teacher and the other is the students. The children may all be different, but in such a class their differences do not count: 'They all have the same things to do, and they are all expected to do them in the same way. Like factory workers on the assembly line, or soldiers in the army, they are interchangeable – and quite often expendable' (*Freedom and Beyond*, p. 11).

A feature of this kind of structure is that it is inflexible, rigid and static. It does not change from the first day of school to the last. On the last day, as on the first, the teacher is giving out information and orders, and the children are passively receiving and obeying or refusing to obey. Such a structure is also arbitrary and external. It does not grow out of the life and needs of the class, what the children want, or what the teacher has to give. It is imposed on them from above. By contrast, the structure of the open class is complicated. It has as many elements as there are teachers and children in the classroom. No two of these elements are alike, and their differences make all the difference, since no two children will relate to the class and teacher, or make use of them, in quite the same way.

This kind of structure is flexible and dynamic. It is organic, and it grows out of the needs and achievements of the children and teachers themselves. They create and develop this order. Children are used to figuring out the rules in complicated human situations, Holt observes, but they do not like a structure that is *contradictory*.

Holt is critical of 'progressive' teachers because they present contradictions for children. They speak the language of freedom, but there are plenty of hidden controls and various hidden agendas. The progressive or so-called 'free' teacher says you can behave any way you like. So, the children have to look for clues, which the adults cannot help giving, to show whether they are doing the right thing or not. This can be exhausting:

> Sometimes the kid gets fed up with it, and like the famous (probably made up) child in the progressive school, says, 'Teacher, do we have to do what we want today?' meaning, do we have to figure out what you want us to do today? Why don't you just tell us? (*Freedom and Beyond*, p. 13)

The vocabulary of freedom creates considerable confusion. One problem arises from the word 'permissive'. This is used as if it is a substitute word for freedom. One result is that when we urge freedom for children or for learners, we find ourselves arguing about whether children should be allowed to do *anything* – torture animals or set buildings on fire. If we say 'No!' we are then told that we don't really believe in freedom after all. Or people say the idea of freedom for children is nonsense; children need limits. All such talk illustrates a great confusion about freedom. It implies that freedom means the absence of any limits or constraints. Holt declares that this is nonsense: 'As there is no life without structure, so there is no life without constraints' (*Freedom and Beyond*, p. 17).

But there are two kinds of restraint, and their consequences are quite different. We can limit choice by insisting that 'You Must Do This'. Or we can say that 'You Must Not Do This'. They are not the same, and are not equally restricting. Telling people what they *may not* do, providing you are clear and specific, allows them much more freedom of choice and action than telling them what they *must* do:

> A free community differs from an unfree one, first, in that its rules are mostly of the Don't Do This rather than the Do This kind, and secondly, that it is clear and specific what you must not do ... What I mean by freedom for children – and for all people – is More Choice, Less Fear. (*Freedom and Beyond*, pp. 19–20)

The freedom to have imaginative play is one that Holt defends at this point. He argues that in their play, children are frequently doing things very much like adults at their work. Like the economist, the traffic engineer, the social planner or the computer expert, children at play often make models of life, or certain parts of life, models they hope are a fair, if simpler, representation of the world, so that by working these models they may attain some idea of how the world works or might work:

More important, what makes our truly inventive and creative thinkers, whether political, artistic, or scientific, what sets them apart from the great run of us, is, above all, that they can still play with their minds. They have not forgotten how to do it, nor grown ashamed, nor afraid of it ... Now we know from experience that out of such play may come, and often do come, ideas that may change the whole shape of human life and thought. (*Freedom and Beyond*, p. 26)

We need *more* imaginative play, not less, Holt concludes, because a society like ours, facing life-or-death crises and predicaments that nobody knows what to do about, and about which most people think nothing at all can be done, needs for its very survival a whole new generation of people who can play with ideas, who can make imaginative leaps.

Freedom brings with it various tensions that many people might call problems. But Holt means something quite different. Tensions cannot be made to go away, because they are built into the nature of things. There are often two conflicting pulls which are both legitimate. They keep on pulling, and so the tension is permanent. When we attempt to put more freedom, autonomy, choice, into children's lives and learning, whether by making a conventional class more open or by starting a new school, some of these tensions will inevitably appear. Holt gives an example of order in classrooms:

Too little, and it is hard to get anything done, or find anything to do. Too much, and we spend more time keeping things orderly than in doing anything with them. Some people are by nature more tolerant of disorder than others. (*Freedom and Beyond*, p. 34)

Holt deals with various other tensions: public and common property, decision making, individual versus community. On the tensions of decision making, he observes that '[e]very time we try to manage the lives of young people, we give up the chance to see how they might have managed their own lives, and to learn what we might have learned from their doing it' (*Freedom and Beyond*, p. 35). The tension between the rights and needs of the individual and of the community can be difficult and painful:

When does the right of one person to live his life cut into the rights of others to live theirs? The point is that neither students nor teachers escape this tension by setting up a school, calling it Free, and saying that they don't have any rules. The tension still exists. (*Freedom and Beyond*, p. 43)

Holt devotes one of the longest chapters in his book to the question of authority. The question of the right relationships between children and adults is itself full of tensions. Holt proposes a rule of thumb:

> If I had to make a general rule for living and working with children, it might be this: be very wary of saying or doing anything to a child that you would not do to another adult, whose good opinion and affection you valued. (*Freedom and Beyond*, p. 51)

On this basis, we ought not to correct the speech of children. This is partly because the children are young, sensitive, easily embarrassed and shamed, and might by too much correction be discouraged from further talking. But there is a much more important reason for not correcting the speech of children. It is a discourtesy, unless asked, to correct the speech of *anyone*. It also weakens the natural propensity to self-correction.

Holt observed that children are less interested in power struggles than is commonly asserted, especially if they are treated with fairness and reason. As a rule, we greatly exaggerate children's interest in power struggles with us. We are so concerned about maintaining our power over them that we think they are equally concerned about taking it away from us:

> They are very much aware that they are powerless, that we have great power over them ... As long as we don't abuse our power intolerably, or weary the children with our constant struggles to assert it, most of them, most of the time, are willing, perhaps even too willing, to accept it. (*Freedom and Beyond*, p. 54)

Our natural authority as adults comes from the fact that we have been in the world longer and seen more of it, and have more words, more skill, more knowledge and more experience. To the extent that our authority is natural, true and authentic, we cannot abdicate it.

This natural authority can quickly become debased, however. The more we intervene in children's lives, however intelligently, kindly or imaginatively, the less time we leave them to find and develop their own competencies and capabilities:

> Many of us may coerce without meaning to. The question is, what kind of influence do we exercise over other people, what kind of open or hidden pressure do we put on them, what chance do we give them to say No, what do they risk if they do say it? (*Freedom and Beyond*, p. 70)

Holt concludes that people in general and children in particular have much greater learning powers than we suspect, and also greater self-curing powers, provided they are given appropriate conditions. Our task is to learn more about these powers, and how we may create conditions in which they may have a chance to work. Choices have to be real.

Holt gives an example of a false choice. One person asks the other, 'Do you believe in God?' After thinking a bit, she says, 'Yes, I suppose so', and then, after a pause, 'After all, what choice do we have?' They live in a culture in which no one would have threatened or punished them for not believing in God. In that sense they were not coerced. But they were surrounded by people who believed or *talked as if* they believed in God, and as if it were important that the children too should believe. Those people would have been most hurt and disappointed if they did not. In effect, they had little choice:

> There is no use in our offering a choice to someone unless we can make him feel that it is a real choice, that he has an equal right to choose either way, that he can do so without having to worry about disappointing us or losing our friendship. (*Freedom and Beyond*, p. 70)

In the chapter 'The Problem of Choice', John Holt opens by reporting the problem that teachers can encounter when they do offer choices to students: the students do not always set about choosing anything or doing anything. Holt is not surprised. First, he tries to see this situation through the eyes of the students. For years they have been playing a school game that looks to them like this: The teacher holds up a hoop and asks them to jump through it. They jump, and if they make it, they get a reward – a smile or praise. The teacher raises the hoop a little higher and again asks them to jump through it. Another jump leads to another reward:

> The rules of the game are simple and clear – hoop, jump, biscuit. Now along comes a teacher who says, 'We aren't going to play that game anymore, you're going to decide for yourselves what you're going to do.' What is the student going to think about this? Almost certainly, he is going to think, 'They're hiding the hoop! It was bad enough having to jump through it before, but now I have to find it.' (*Freedom and Beyond*, p. 77)

The offer of freedom, choice or self-direction to students who have spent much time in traditional schools is not instantly taken up. They do not trust the offer or believe us. Given their experience, Holt explains, they are quite right not to. Students in a traditional school learn before long in a hundred different ways that the school is not on their side. It is working not for them, but for the community and the state; it is not interested in them except insofar as they serve its purposes; and that among all the reasons for which the adults in the school do things, the learners' happiness, health and growth are by far the least important. The offer itself may be a sleight of hand trick. Many parents, and more than a few educators, have seized on the idea of the open classroom, freedom and choice, not as a way of having students direct their own learning, explore the world in the way that seems best to them, but only as a way of getting them to do conventional schoolwork more willingly and hence more rapidly than before.

Lack of trust in us is not the only reason why students may be slow to use the freedom and choice we offer them. If the students decide that our offer is genuine, there is another problem. They may not trust themselves enough to be willing to choose. We should not be surprised at this, because they have been taught in school, in the unwritten curriculum as well as the official one, to distrust themselves. This is one of the few things that schools teach well:

> To choose is to risk. We must realize that when we ask or invite them to make choices we are asking them to take a risk much larger than the risks we have spent years teaching them never to take. No wonder many of them hang back. (*Freedom and Beyond*, p. 82)

Holt reports on the experience he had described in *What Do I Do Monday?* (see Chapter 6), where he taught at the Harvard Graduate School of Education a one-semester course called Student-Directed Learning. At the first meeting he talked about how he saw the course and what he planned to do in it. He had a certain amount of resources and experiences, all having to do with student-directed or open learning, that he was going to put before them. The class seemed to think his offer and plan were reasonable. Then at one class meeting there was an explosion. They said that he did not care about them, otherwise he would tell them what to do. He said that he did care about them; that was why he did not want to tell them what to do. If it were true, and it seemed to be, that many of them had never had the chance to decide for themselves whether to read a book or not, write a paper or not, go to a meeting or not, then he proposed that it was time they began making decisions.

It follows that it is dubious to talk of 'giving freedom' to people. The most we can do is lay on certain choices, and remove some coercions and constraints. Whether doing this creates for other people something they recognize as a release, liberation, opportunity, freedom, or whether it just puts them in a more painful spot than ever, is very much up to them and how they have come to see things. It may help to start gradually: 'When we first try to open up our classrooms it may make the change easier for everyone if instead of offering a wide choice from the start, we widen the range of choice very gradually' (*Freedom and Beyond*, p. 87). Giving students choices may generate opposition from other quarters such as parents or other colleagues. They may take a up a strong negative attitude: 'Don't give these kids (my kids) ideas; they'll just get them in trouble. Teach them to keep their mouths shut, their noses clean, and to do what they're told. That way they'll get along fine' (*Freedom and Beyond*, p. 98). In this situation it may be better to retreat and look for another school. Some radical student teachers are unrealistic in thinking that their duty is to find an authoritarian and rigid school and, by teaching in it and struggling with it, to try to make it more humane. Holt suggests that the task may well be impossible, and that they will just get themselves into trouble and probably fired.

Sooner or later, the idea of freedom raises the question of discipline:

When people talk about their child 'learning discipline', what is it that they really want him to learn? Probably, most or all of the following:

1. Do what you're told without questioning or resisting, whenever I or any other authority tell you to do something.
2. Go on doing what you're told for as long as you're told. Never mind how dull, disagreeable, or pointless the task may seem. It's not for you to decide.
3. Do whatever we want you to do, *willingly*. Do it without even having to be told. Do what you're expected to do.
4. If you don't do these things you will be punished and you will deserve to be.
5. Accept your life without complaining, even if you get very little of any of what you think you want, even if your life has not much joy, meaning, or satisfaction. That's what life is.
6. Take your medicine, your punishment, whatever the people above you do to you, without complaining or resisting.
7. Living this way is good for your soul and character. (*Freedom and Beyond*, p. 100)

The rich and powerful, Holt observes, always like to tell the poor and lowly about the virtues of duty, obedience and hard work, since it serves their interests. They want more coercion, more threats, more punishment, more fear – above all, more fear.

Holt distinguishes three kinds of discipline. The first, and perhaps the most important, is what we might call the Discipline of Nature or of Reality: if you hit the wrong key, you hear the wrong note. The second is the Discipline of Culture, of Society, of What People Really Do:

The little children that I see at concerts or operas, though they may fidget a little, or perhaps take a nap now and then, rarely make any disturbance.

With all those grown-ups sitting there, neither moving or talking, it is the most natural thing in the world to imitate them. (*Freedom and Beyond*, p. 103)

The third discipline is the one most people mean when they speak of discipline: the Discipline of Superior Force. This one should be used very sparingly, for it is never good for anyone's character:

To bow to superior force makes us feel impotent and cowardly for not having had the strength or courage to resist. Worse, it makes us resentful and vengeful. We can hardly wait to make someone pay for our humiliation, yield to us as we were once made to yield. No, if we cannot always avoid using the Discipline of Superior Force, we should at least use it as seldom as we can. (*Freedom and Beyond*, p. 104)

Another chapter is entitled 'Beyond Schooling'. In it Holt records his answer to an African visitor who surprised him with this question: 'If I were to take back to my country a message about education, what do you think it should be?' The reply was 'My message to your countrymen might be that you don't have to have school buildings in order to have schools and you don't have to have schools in order to have education' (*Freedom and Beyond*, p. 116).

Holt declares that an ideal system would not have schools at all. He imagines that he is traveling into the future in a time capsule and that he comes to rest five hundred years from now in an intelligent, humane and life-enhancing civilization. One of the people who lives there comes to meet him and to explain the society. At some point, after he has been shown where people live, work, play, Holt asks:

'But where are your schools?'
   'Schools? What are schools?' he replies.
   'Schools are places where people go to learn things.'
   'I do not understand,' he says. 'People learn things everywhere, in all places.'
   'I know that,' I say. 'But a school is a special place where there are special people who teach you things, help you learn things.'
   'I am sorry, but I still do not understand. Everyone helps other people learn things. Anyone who knows something or can do something can help someone else who wants to learn more about it. Why should there be special people to do this?'
   And try as I will, I cannot make clear to him why we think that education should be, must be, separate from the rest of life. (*Freedom and Beyond*, p. 117)

Yet almost all societies and people now *define* education or learning as schooling, and measure people's intelligence, competence, job worthiness and capacity for further learning in terms of the length in years and the expense of the schooling they have already received.

Most students in US universities turn out to be the children of university graduates, and this has nothing to do with intelligence or ability. School is a very special world and the school game a very special game, and people who like that world and play that game well will probably have children who do the same, just as the children of musicians are likely to be musicians, or the children of circus people are likely to work in circuses.

There is an opportunity cost:

> Another consequence of defining education as schooling is that as we put more and more of our educational resources into schools, we have less and less left over for those institutions that are truly open and educative and in which more and more people might learn for themselves. One example would be the public libraries. (*Freedom and Beyond*, p. 127)

Holt devotes a large section of his book to the themes of 'Schooling and Poverty' and 'Deschooling and the Poor'. He exposes a series of myths about how schooling serves the poor. The link between school and the economy is weak. The number of jobs that exist, and the goodness or badness of these jobs and the amount of money they pay, is independent of the schools, of the things they teach there, and of the number of people who are learning in them. Schools can only react to this situation. The dominant fact is that

> the comfortable and pleasant and powerful places in society are *occupied*, and the people who are in those places are not going to move out of them and down in society just so that poor people can move up and in. (*Freedom and Beyond*, p. 185)

Therefore, the message 'Work hard in school, do better than all these other children, get that degree, and you'll make it in society!' is true for only a very few. The majority will be kept firmly in their poverty. Holt sees that schools and schooling, by their very nature, purposes, structure and ways of working, are, and are meant to be, an obstacle to poorer children, designed and built not to move them up in the world but to keep them at the bottom of it and to make them think it is their own fault. The odds against not just all poor children but any poor child being helped rather than hurt by school are enormous. For the parents of poor children to put all their hopes into getting good schooling for their children seems to Holt to have about as much chance of paying off as putting all their money into sweepstakes.

Meanwhile, Holt suggests that we are stuck with old bad habits, old ways of thought, and the deadly consequences of what we are doing, and not just in education. Republican presidents have been known to declare that they were not going to change the American economic system and its fixation with market forces no matter what it might do to our environment: 'Not only do we not know how to save Earth, our planet, our home, our spaceship, our mother; we are not really sure we care enough even to want to save it' (*Freedom and Beyond*, p. 159).

Alternatives are not welcome news. John Holt knew Denmark quite well and visited it from time to time. The Danes maintain a standard of living close to that of the USA on only about one twentieth of the resources consumed per person, by operating a more cooperative rather than an open-war competitive system. But there is no desire in the USA to learn from this example:

> But their average standard of living, even measured in strictly economic terms, is close to ours; in less economic terms, it may well be higher. And thirty million or so Americans are poorer than the poorest Dane, and live in a squalor and misery that they would not put up with. (*Freedom and Beyond*, p. 177)

Holt goes on to say that in the USA, much of the GNP serves no need at all, other than the need for job, career, status, wealth and power on the part of those who provide it. Nobody *wants* to read advertising or to see TV commercials. Few people would have asked to pay, or if asked would have agreed to pay, for the space program, the hydrogen bomb, nuclear submarines, or the Vietnam War, to name only a few massive wasteful projects.

Schooling is just another wasteful and expensive project that favors the rich. As fast as poor children learn to run the school obstacle course, already much longer and tougher for them than for those of the middle class, ways will be found to make the course still longer. It is a great way, among other things, of burning off the political energies and anger of the poor. We can keep them busy for years scrambling and competing against each other for a scarce handful of degrees, on the chance that they may then get jobs that, in most cases, could have been done just as well without the degrees. Nor are poor children free from discrimination even when they get the degrees, Holt observes. They still need the connections to become successful. Where before they had to run one obstacle course, now they have to run another.

The irony is that the carrot offered is to 'become like us' – the people who are wasteful and greedy – by destroying your identity. Defenders of schools constantly asked Holt whether he would want to be operated on by a doctor without any training, or willing to cross a bridge built by someone without any training, etc. Of course not ... But it certainly did not matter to him whether the person who removes the appendix, builds the bridge to be crossed or whatever, said 'ain't' or did not speak Standard English, wore funny clothes or haircuts, or shared the same tastes in books and music.

But these are the things the schools think they have to teach *first*, and the children who do not learn them, or refuse to learn them, or pretend not to learn them, are never allowed to get far enough up the school ladder to have a chance to learn how to take out appendixes or build bridges. In short, what schools demand of poor children, as a condition of being given a chance to learn some skills that might get them into the middle class, is that they act as if they were already in it.

Some justify schools on the grounds that the students are likely to be learning *something*. Even if they are, they will not remember more than a fraction of it, or use or benefit from more than a small part of that. They are only learning this stuff to pass exams. Most of them could not pass the same exam even a year later, to say nothing of ten years later. They need a much freer, less restricted, less expensive access to what opportunities there are in society. Above all, they need a society in which there are many more opportunities, a society committed to doing away with poverty and to making available and possible an active, interesting and useful life to all its members. These are, above all, political needs, ends and goals. None of them is something that schools and schooling can provide.

In the section 'Reading without Schooling', Holt suggests that learning to read without school might be a more successful venture, and he quotes the case of Paulo Freire. Northeastern Brazil is one of the great poverty areas of the world. Most of the people are tenant farmers or sharecroppers. They own nothing. They must pay even for the water they get from the landlord's well. They live in poverty, in isolated villages. They have none of the books, newspapers, signs or TV advertising that surround almost all children in modern society. Yet Paulo Freire and colleagues trained by him were able to teach large numbers of wholly illiterate adults in these villages to write and read in a few months, and at a cost of $25 per person:

When Freire and his co-workers came into a new village their first step was to try to get the villagers to come together in a meeting, to discuss their lives, interests, needs, problems, and concerns. Many people were afraid (like many people in the United States) that if they spoke out in public they would get in some kind of trouble. Many more felt that since nothing they said could make any difference in their lives, what was the use of saying anything? Why even think? Better live out your short and wretched life in a kind of numbed resignation. Freire describes the culture in which such people live (the culture of poverty is in a sense world-wide) as the Culture of Silence. Words are not used because they would be wasted. (*Freedom and Beyond*, p. 218)

But as they talked, they gained courage, and began to speak with passion and conviction. Certain words began to appear, key words that Freire calls 'generative' words – they generate ideas, and they generate syllables out of which other words can be made. Freire would write these words down and show the villagers how to write them. Once they reached this point, the rest followed. They were able to help these villagers become functionally literate in evening classes after a hard day's work, over a period of about eight weeks. All this took place without schools of the current model:

> His 'schools' were altogether different from the schools we know and have, and that I and others, in our talk of deschooling, want to get away from. In the first place, they were not compulsory. In the second, they neither required nor gave any credentials. In the third, they did not lock the student into a prescribed sequence of learning determined in advance. (*Freedom and Beyond*, p. 219)

Reflecting on Freire's success led Holt to the idea of the volunteer reading guide. The guides would wear some kind of identification – an armband, hat or something similar, so that people wanting information could easily spot them. When guides were wearing the sign, anyone who wanted could ask them one of two kinds of question. The person could show a written word and ask, 'What does this say?' and the guide would give the answer. Or the person could say to the guide, 'How do you write such and such a word?' and the guide would write it down. That is all a guide would have to do. Reading guides would not have to do their guiding all the time, only as much of the time as they wanted, fitting it in along with the rest of their life. We can, of course, easily exaggerate the role of reading in our culture:

> From the fuss we make about reading, one might think that this was a country of readers, that reading was nearly everyone's favorite or near-favorite pastime. Who are we kidding? A publisher told me not long ago that outside of three hundred or so college bookstores, there are less than one hundred true bookstores in all the United States. (*Freedom and Beyond*, p. 229)

Finally, in 'Schools against Themselves' Holt tackles the puzzle of why schools resist change so persistently. After all, people have been working at reforming schools for years. Not many of the ideas of today's school reformers are new. This is not the first time people have talked about the need for a new, more humane vision:

A large number of our schools are joyless, repressive, mindless. What is
puzzling, though, is why they are and why they resist so well efforts to
make them something else. Why is it so hard for schools to move forward,
and so easy to slip back? (*Freedom and Beyond*, p. 238)

Visiting schools systems and talking with school people in many different
parts of the country, Holt often heard about interesting new programs. But
just about as often, he heard another story about how they had had a good
program going a few years previously, running the schools in a more flexible,
interesting and humane way, using new materials, or breaking free of the old
patterns, or getting out of the building. The students were really excited,
really happy, really learning. But then, apparently, something happened.
The parents complained. The money ran out. The superintendent left for
another job, or was fired. Or a new school board was elected. Or the teachers
did not like the program any more and whittled it down. And so things would
go back to the way they always were.

Clearly, some of the people running schools or teaching in them are people who ought not to be there. They do not like or trust children. They do
not like their work with them. They see their main task as getting children
ready for a life and work that they themselves find dull, pointless and oppressive. This means that the percentage of really good schools – enlightened,
flexible, humane, inspired and inspiring, exciting, life enhancing – remains
low, so much lower than the percentage of school people who would wish
schools to be like that. But the basic reason is compulsion:

I think the answer is plain enough, and that we would see it if we did
not keep turning our heads away from it. Universal compulsory schools
are not and never were meant to be humane institutions, and most of
their fundamental purposes, tasks, missions, are not humane. (*Freedom
and Beyond*, p. 242)

The rhetoric says that there is one prime, legitimate, humane mission or
function of the schools: to promote the growth of the children in them. We
can call this the educative mission. But schools as they currently exist have
other missions and other functions. In this he echoes a point that Winston
Churchill had made before him: 'Schools have not necessarily much to do
with education ... they are mainly institutions of control where certain basic
habits must be instilled in the young. Education is quite different and has
little place in school' (*Freethinkers' Guide to the Educational Universe, a Selection
of Quotations*, Nottingham: Educational Heretics Press, p. 77). Churchill did
not go on to say what should be done about it; that was left to later analysts
such as Holt, Illich, Reimer, Papert and Taylor-Gatto. One of the missions of

schools is the custodial function. Schools operate as places where for many hours of the day, many days of the year, children or young people can be confined to get them out of everyone else's way. Most mothers do not want them hanging around the house, most citizens do not want them out in the streets, and most workers do not want them in the labor force. Therefore, we put them in schools. That is an important part of what schools are for. They are a kind of day prison for children:

> This task or function of schools, the custodial or jail function, the task of keeping young people out of everybody else's way, is quite obviously not a humane function. It is an expression of adults' general dislike and distrust of the young. It is and must be in conflict with the humane function of true education, of encouraging and helping human growth. (*Freedom and Beyond*, p. 244)

The schools have another important function. It is social role selection. We might also call it grading and labeling. If we want to be blunt, Holt says, we might call it meat stamping:

> The channeling function, the task of separating the winners from losers may be a needed and proper function somewhere, but it is improper and inhumane in the schools. The things we do to select a few winners defeat whatever things we do to encourage the growth of all. We cannot do both of these kinds of work at the same time, in the same place. We cannot in any true sense be in the education business and at the same time in the grading and labeling business. (*Freedom and Beyond*, p. 250)

Yet another important function of the schools is indoctrination. This means getting the children to think whatever the adults, or at least politically powerful adults, think, or want the children to think. Some of this indoctrination is straightforward and direct. One example is 'patriotism': 'It is the patriotism of Admiral Decatur, who, they tell us (not quite accurately) first spoke the famous words, "My country, right or wrong"' (*Freedom and Beyond*, p. 251). But there is another version of this dictum that is hardly ever used. It is that of Carl Schurz, a German immigrant boy who later became mayor of New York, and who replied, 'My country, right or wrong; if right, to be kept right; if wrong, to be put right' (*Freedom and Beyond*, p. 251).

Holt notes that our society also wants to pass on to children certain beliefs about such assorted matters as sex, morality, corporate enterprise and the profit system. We are trained to sell our learning for grades so that later we will sell our work for money. Worse, we learn to think not only that work is what we do for money, out of fear, envy or greed, but also that work is what we would never do *except* for money, that there could be no other reason to work, that anyone who talks about meaningful work must be the wildest kind of romantic dreamer and crackpot. We learn to take it as natural, right and inevitable that our work should be boring, meaningless, hateful.

In order to achieve these non-educative functions, schools are compelled to mount an unrelenting and merciless attack on the dignity and self-respect of the students. Schools do not have the power of life and death over children, but they do have the power to cause them mental and physical pain, to threaten, frighten and humiliate them, and to destroy their future lives. This power has been enough to corrupt deeply many schools and school people, to turn many a teacher into a cruel and petty tyrant even though he or she did not start out to be one and might even now not want to be one. If there were no other reasons for schools to rid themselves of this power, this would be enough. Only by doing so can the schools save their own souls.

Chapter 8

Escape from Childhood

It was reading Paul Goodman's *Growing Up Absurd* (New York: Random House, 1960) that started John Holt reflecting seriously about whether childhood was such a good idea. In the opening chapter of *Escape from Childhood*, Holt defines the problem of being a 'child' as that of being wholly subservient and dependent, of being seen by older people as a mixture of expensive nuisance, slave and superpet.

This role does most young people more harm than good, so Holt proposes radical changes so that the rights, privileges, duties, responsibilities of adult citizens be made available to any young person, of whatever age, who wants to make use of them. These would include, among others:

1. The right to equal treatment at the hands of the law – i.e., the right, in any situation, to be treated no worse than an adult would be.
2. The right to vote, and take full part in political affairs.
3. The right to be legally responsible for one's life and acts.
4. The right to work, for money.
5. The right to privacy.
6. The right to financial independence and responsibility – i.e., the right to own, buy, and sell property, to borrow money, establish credit, sign contracts etc.
7. The right to direct and manage one's own education.
8. The right to travel, to live away from home, to choose or make one's own home.
9. The right to receive from the state whatever minimum income it may guarantee to adult citizens.
10. The right to make and enter into, on a basis of mutual consent, quasi-familial relationships outside one's immediate family – i.e., the right to seek and choose guardians other than one's own parents and to be legally dependent on them.
11. The right to do, in general, what any adult may legally do. (*Escape from Childhood*, p. 15)

Holt's list is not compiled in any order of importance, because what some young people might find most important, others would find less so. The list is not a package deal, so a young person does not have to assume all of them, or for that matter any of them, if he or she does not wish to. People should be able to pick and choose.

Such changes could not come about all at once. If they ever take place, it will be as a process, a series of steps taken over a number of years. Holt is aware, of course, that these ideas may seem reckless or eccentric. He is unperturbed:

> No state of affairs is permanently perfect. Cures for old evils sooner or later create new ones. The most and best we can do is to try to change and cure what we know is wrong right now and deal with new evils as they come up. (*Escape from Childhood*, p. 18)

The kind of country needed for such changes is hard to find. What Holt proposed could well take place, he said, in any reasonably intelligent, honest, kindly and humane country in which, on the whole, people do not need and do not crave power over others, do not worry much about being number one, do not live under the constant threat of severe poverty, uselessness and failure, do not exploit and prey upon each other.

Holt turns his attention to the institution of childhood. It has its roots in ageism, in all the attitudes and feelings, and also customs and laws, that put a great gulf or barrier between the young and their elders and create two separate worlds, making it difficult or impossible for young people to make contact with the larger society around them, and, even more, to play any kind of active, responsible, useful part in it. Ageism locks the young into 18 years of subserviency and dependency, and defines them as a mixture of fragile treasure and problem. Most people who believe in the institution of childhood as we know it see it as a kind of walled garden in which children, being small and weak, are protected from the harshness of the world outside until they become strong and clever enough to cope with it. Some children experience childhood in just that way. Holt did not want to destroy their garden or kick them out of it. If they like it, by all means let them stay in it, he thought:

> But I believe that most young people, and at earlier and earlier ages, begin to experience childhood not as a garden but as a prison. What I want to do is put a gate, or gates, into the wall of the garden, so that those who find it no longer protective or helpful, but instead confining and humiliating, can move out of it and for a while try living in a larger space. If that proves too much for them, they can always come back into the garden. (*Escape from Childhood*, p. 22)

Holt is not saying that childhood is bad for all children all the time. But Childhood, as in Happy, Safe, Protected, Innocent Childhood, is just a myth for many children. For many other children, however good it may be, childhood goes on far too long, and there is no gradual, sensible and painless way to grow out of it or leave it.

Childhood is a modern invention. Holt points out that children's toys did not appear until around 1600 and even then were not used beyond the age of 3 or 4. In the late seventeenth century there is the introduction of special children's games, but childhood did not apply to women, for the female child went from swaddling clothes right into adult female dress. She did not go to school, which was the institution that later structured childhood. At the age of 9 or 10 she acted, literally, like a 'little lady'; her activity did not differ from that of adult women. As soon as she reached puberty, as early as 10 or 12, she was married off to a much older male. Children were involved in adult life until more recent times, partly because there was no way to keep them out. Poor people, of course, had, then as now, so little space in which to live that children had to see and know about all the realities of life:

> We constantly ask ourselves, in anxiety and pain, 'What is best for the children, what is right for the children, what should we do for the children?' The question is an effect as well as a cause of modern childhood. Until the institution was invented, it would hardly have occurred to anybody to ask the question or, if they had, to suppose that what was good for children was any different from what was good for everyone else. (*Escape from Childhood*, p. 32)

At its best, the family can be an island of acceptance and love in the midst of a harsh world. But too often within the family people take out on each other all the pain and frustrations of their lives that they do not dare take out on anyone else.

Holt devotes space to the issue of the loss of authority of the older generation. He dismisses the idea that this is related to 'being too soft' and instead follows the Alice Miller thesis:

> We know that many of our most unruly young, in or out of schools, the ones who most fiercely and violently defy all authority, who form gangs and commit crimes, are those who in their early years were most strictly and punitively brought up. (*Escape from Childhood*, p. 44)

Rapid change has contributed to a loss of confidence for a generation that does not believe it can make a future that it will like or trust, and has nothing to pass on to the young:

It might seem a paradox that our society, which perhaps more than any that ever existed, is obsessed with the need to control events, nature, people, everything, should feel more than any other, that things are out of control. But it is not a paradox; like a drowning man we clutch frantically at any fragments of certainty we can make or reach. (*Escape from Childhood*, p. 46)

Not many people believe anymore that the place they live in, be it city, town, neighborhood, or country, will be a better place in ten years' time. The most they dare hope for is that they will be able to hold off disaster for a while and that when disaster comes, they will be rich enough to escape to some new, unspoiled or less spoiled place and live in it for a while until it too is spoiled.

The gap that has been created between childhood and the rest of life is only one of a number of growing gaps. For all our talk about 'senior citizens', old age is defined for many as a useless time of life. Nobody wants you, nobody is interested in you, you are a bother and a nuisance, you cannot do anything, and you do not know anything that is seen as worth knowing. Indeed, we are more and more coming to think of human life as a series of crises: the crisis of puberty, the crisis of adolescence, the crisis of middle age, the crisis of old age. It is almost as if the only age to be is between 21 and 35.

Inventing childhood has also made having children a burden:

Modern childhood is an extraordinary emotional and financial burden. And as this burden has become heavier beyond anyone's wildest imagining, parents have been told ever more insistently that they have a *duty* to love their children, and the children that they have a duty to love their parents. (*Escape from Childhood*, p. 55)

It follows that bringing up children now is for many people an endless worry. There is no legitimate way for parents, staggering under this burden, to admit without shame or guilt that they do not much like these young people who live in their house, worry them half to death and soak up most of their money, or that they wish they had never decided to have them in the first place, or that they could have had something different. The children, on their part, are expected to be grateful for what they did not ask for and often do not want.

Holt makes a prophecy derived from this situation, which has certainly come true in the UK in my lifetime, and also, I am told by my correspondents, in the USA too: 'A majority want the schools to be even more rigid, threatening, and punitive than they are, and they will probably become so' (*Escape from Childhood*, p. 58).

Holt notes that children meet one need of many adults: the need to have someone to control. Adult parents, however lowly or powerless, have at least someone that they can command, threaten and punish:

> And so the family home, which we often hear described as the place where we are free to be and dare to be nicer and kinder than we can be anywhere else, turns out much of the time to be the place where at least to our children we can be harsher, more cruel, more contemptuous and insulting, than we would be anywhere else. (*Escape from Childhood*, p. 60)

Holt moves on to consider how the idea of help becomes corrupted and turned into a destructive exploitation, how the human act of helping is turned more and more into a commodity, an industry and a monopoly. He is troubled by people who want to make a lifework out of being, usually without being asked, the helper and protector of others, because unless they are very careful they are almost certain to define them as people who cannot get along without this help. If this happens, helpers feed and thrive on helplessness:

> The trouble with the helping professions – teaching, psychiatry, psychology, social work – is that they tend to attract people who want to play God. Some of them, perhaps most of them, want to play a kindly and benevolent God; others, and perhaps without knowing it, may want to play a harsh and cruel God. (*Escape from Childhood*, p. 62)

Holt insists on the right to make mistakes, for most people in the course of their lives will make plenty of mistakes. He observes that, given real choices and alternatives, most people will manage their lives better than anyone else, however expert. In any case, the only way we can fully protect people against their own mistakes is to make them slaves. They are then defenceless before our whims and weaknesses. Most people would prefer to take their chances with the world, and they have the right to that choice.

Holt considers the competence of children and also what adult anxiety does to children. This contains messages that tell the young both about themselves and about the world around them, and their ability to cope with it. It tells them that (1) the world is a terribly dangerous, treacherous, unpredictable place, and (2) you are wholly unable to cope with it and must depend on adults to keep you out of all kinds of trouble. Such expectations often become self-fulfilling prophecies. The words 'expect' and 'expectation' are on the whole badly misunderstood and misused by most people who write about children. Most people use them as synonyms for 'demand' or 'insist' or 'compel'. When they say we should have higher expectations of children, they mean that we would demand that they do certain things and threaten to punish them if they do not:

> When I speak of expecting a lot of children, I only mean that we should not in our minds put an upper limit on what they may be able to do. I don't mean we should assume that they can, and therefore should, do certain things or be disappointed and worried if they do not – everyone has his own path and timetable into life. (*Escape from Childhood*, p. 74)

Apart from children serving the need to have someone to control, they also serve the need for a love object. Adults tend to think that they have a right, or even a duty, to bestow on them 'love', visible and tangible signs of affection, whenever they want, however they want, and whether the young like it or not. In this way, adults exploit them, use them for their purposes. This, more than anything else, is what adults use children and childhood for: to provide them with love objects. This is why adults find children worth owning and the institution of childhood worth preserving, in spite of their great trouble and expense.

Holt is keen to point out that this does not mean that our desire to love children is bad, or all bad. People are right to be interested, charmed and delighted by many qualities of children with their energy, enthusiasm, health, quickness, boisterousness, curiosity, intelligence, gaiety, spontaneity, vivacity, intensity, passion, expressiveness, hopefulness, trustfulness, playfulness, generosity, magnanimity, and above all their great capacity for wonder and delight. It is right to be touched and saddened by their littleness, weakness, inexperience, ignorance, clumsiness, vulnerability, and lack of all sense of time and proportion. But this gives adults no right to indulge these feelings, to wallow in them to make us feel good:

> But we should not think of these qualities or virtues as 'childish', the exclusive property of children. They are human qualities. We are wise to value them in people of all ages. When we think of these qualities as childish, belonging only to children, we invalidate them. (*Escape from Childhood*, p. 85)

Much of what we respond to in children as 'sweet' or 'cute' is not strength but weakness, a quality that gives us power over them or helps us to feel superior. We may think they are sweet partly because they are little. But what is sweet about being little? Midgets are not cute, for we recognize that the littleness of a midget is an affliction and a burden.

Holt develops his point by analyzing the idea of the 'innocence' of children. This frequently means that they are ignorant and inexperienced. Such ignorance is not to be admired; it is a misfortune. Children acting really competently and intelligently do not usually strike us as cute. Children do not like being incompetent any more than they like being ignorant. They want to learn how to do, and do well, the things they see being done by bigger people around them. This is why they soon find school such a disappointment; they so seldom get a chance to learn anything important or do anything real: 'But many of the defenders of childhood, in or out of school, seem to have this vested interest in the children's incompetence, which they often call "letting the child be a child"' (*Escape from Childhood*, p. 92).

Paradoxically, many parents have a plan for moving their children on from innocence. Having turned children into an ideal abstraction, many parents and teachers tend to look at them much as Mission Control in Houston looks at a moon shot. They have a trajectory (life) all mapped out for children, and they are constantly monitoring them to see whether they are on the path or whether they need a little boost from one rocket (psychologist) here or a sideways push from another rocket (learning specialist) there. Are they on course? Are they on schedule?

In a section entitled 'Love May Not Cure Everything', Holt considers that there may be some lost causes and that people who have already developed a destructive outlook may be just too difficult to help. Even schools that reach out to such children can fail. It is possible to fail as completely at a free or alternative school like Summerhill or Lewis-Wadhams or First Street School as at the most rigid and conventional school. In a school whose main work is having everyone get good marks in exams, whoever cannot do this is a failure. But in a school whose main work is helping everyone to be happy, to love and be loved, anyone who cannot do this is just as much a failure.

The best way to escape childhood is to grow up, and while they are growing up, children want to be around the kind of adults who like being grown up and who think of growing up as an exploration and adventure, not the process of being chased out of some garden of Eden. They do not want to 'experience childhood', which means that adults will decide, without often or ever asking children what they think, that some experiences are good for children while others are not.

Neither do they need 'time to grow'. The child is going to grow whether people 'give' time or not. If we want children to grow not just in age, size and strength, but in understanding, awareness, kindness, confidence, competence and joy, then they need not time as such, but access to experiences that will build these other qualities.

Therefore, to help children escape childhood, we should give them more rights. In granting us rights, the law does not say what we must or shall do. It simply says that it will not allow other people to prevent us from doing those things. The right to manage their own learning comes first. Young people should have the right to control and direct their own learning – that is, to decide what they want to learn, and when, where, how, how much, how fast and with what help they want to learn it. To be still more specific, Holt wants them to have the right to decide whether, when, how much and by whom they want to be *taught*, and the right to decide whether they want to learn in a school, and if so which one, and for how much of the time. It is a matter of human rights. Holt concludes that no human right, except the right to life itself, is more fundamental than this. Freedom of learning is part of freedom of thought, even more basic than freedom of speech. If we take from people the right to decide what they will be curious about, we destroy their freedom of thought. We impose the view that you must think not about what interests and concerns *you*, but what interests and concerns *us*:

> When we put into our laws the highly authoritarian notion that someone should and could decide what all young people were to learn and, beyond that, could do whatever might seem necessary (which now includes dosing them with drugs) to compel them to learn it, we took a long step down a very steep and dangerous path. The requirement that a child go to school, for about six hours a day, 180 days a year, for about ten years, whether or not he learns anything there, whether or not he already knows it or could learn it faster or better somewhere else, is such a gross violation of civil liberties that few adults would stand for it. But the child who resists is treated as a criminal. The right I ask for the young is a right that I want to preserve for the rest of us, *the right to decide what goes into our minds*. (*Escape from Childhood*, p. 184)

To say that children should have the right to control and direct their own learning, to go to school or not as they choose, does not mean that the law should forbid the parents from expressing an opinion or wish or strong desire on the matter. It only means that if their natural authority is not strong enough, the parents cannot call in the police to make the child do what they are not able to persuade him or her to do.

Schools, Holt had come to see, were worse than most of the people in them, and many of these people do many harmful things they would rather not do, and a great many other harmful things that they do not even see as harmful. The whole of the school is much worse than the sum of its parts. There are very few people in the USA today (or perhaps anywhere, at any time) in *any* occupation who could be trusted with the kind of power that schools give most teachers over their students. Schools are among the most anti-democratic, most authoritarian, most destructive and most dangerous institutions of modern society. No other institution does more harm or more lasting harm to more people or destroys so much of their curiosity, independence, trust, dignity and sense of identity and worth. Even quite kindly schools are inhibited and corrupted by the knowledge of both children and teachers that they are *performing* for the judgment and approval of others: the children for the teachers, the teachers for the parents, supervisors, school board or the state.

They are at least as bad as the world outside, and the harm they do to the children in their power sustains and even creates much of the badness of the world outside. The sickness of the modern world is in many ways a school-induced sickness. It is in school that most people learn to expect and accept that some expert can always place them in some sort of rank or hierarchy. It is in school that we meet, become used to, and learn to believe in the totally controlled society.

Both power and powerlessness corrupt people. Powerlessness gives them the mind and soul of slaves. It makes them indifferent, lazy, cynical, irresponsible and, above all, stupid.

Holt them turns his attention to the issue of voting. Nelson Mandela vowed to make 14 the voting age in the new South Africa, because people as young as this fought and gave their lives for the right to vote in the struggle against apartheid. It was first of all a matter of justice, because if someone is going to be affected by what you decide, they should have a say in it. Furthermore, to deny the vote to the young is all the more unjust because they are likely to be more deeply affected than anyone else by the decisions the government makes and the things it does. They will have to live longer with the consequences of what is done and any mistakes that are made.

But Holt is not overimpressed by the right to vote:

That every so often the people in power have to make some kind of report to the voters, and get some kind of endorsement for what they have done or want to do, is obviously not much of a check on them. But it is better than no check at all. (*Escape from Childhood*, p. 118)

The idea of giving younger people the vote is not a popular cause:

When I say that very young people should be allowed to vote, many [people] react with fear and anger. At one meeting a man rose, voice shaking, and asked me what made me think – he could hardly get the words out – how could I imagine that a six-year-old child would know enough to know what to do about inflation. I said, 'The President of the United States doesn't know what to do about inflation. Neither do the heads of state of any other countries that I know of'. (*Escape from Childhood*, p. 126)

The idea that adult voters are well informed is, in any case, nonsense, Holt reminds us. Surveys show that most US people (in spite of their schooling) do not even *recognize* the Declaration of Independence or the Bill of Rights when they are typed out on ordinary paper and shown to them. When they are asked to sign these statements, the most fundamental documents of US society and supposedly the foundation of that country's political system, about nine out of ten people refuse, calling them radical, subversive or communist.

Yet, no amount of ignorance, or outright delusion, is held to be a reason for preventing an adult from voting. There are still people around who believe that the Earth is flat, or hollow; yet they can vote. Many still believe in a literal interpretation of the Bible, that the world was created in seven days or that woman was created from man's rib, and so on; yet they can vote:

> There is simply no way in which we could devise a proper test for voters or insure that it would be used fairly and not to the benefit of whoever happened to control the election machinery. The only answer is to give the vote to everyone who wants it, do all we can to see that they have access to information that will help them vote wisely and hope for the best. (*Escape from Childhood*, p. 130)

Holt now turns his attention to another highly charged issue, that of drugs. He proposes that whatever rights the law grants to adults in the matter of drugs should be granted to the young. On the whole, Holt believed that people ought to be able to use the drugs they want. Those who sell drugs should be made by law to say what is in them and whatever is known about the short- and long-term effects of the drug. Therefore, a requirement that sellers of tobacco say on each package that smoking may be injurious to your health does not seem nearly strong enough. It ought to say clearly that the evidence shows that smoking over a number of years will greatly increase one's chances of getting heart attacks, emphysema, and cancer of the mouth, throat or lungs:

> We were a drug culture long before the young started using drugs of their own and getting known for it. Most adults are regular and even heavy users of at least three psychoactive drugs – coffee, tobacco, and alcohol ... We might even add a fourth chemical to this list – sugar ... most of our population, including children, are badly hooked on it ... many adults take large amounts of other drugs. Millions are chronic users of aspirin, tranquillisers, pep pills, diet pills, sleeping pills. (*Escape from Childhood*, pp. 191–2)

Holt has something to say about the right to drive. He suggest that tests for a driver's license should be made harder, that people should have to take them more often, and that people should much more easily than now, and for a wider range of driving offenses, lose their licenses. But anyone, of whatever age, who can show that he or she has the knowledge and skill to drive a car safely and well, ought to be allowed to drive it. A minimum age is not necessary.

Finally, Holt takes on the contentious issue of the law, the young and sex. His first plea is for open access to information about sex, arguing that if by the age of 10 all young people knew how pregnancies occur and how they can be prevented, if birth control materials and advice were widely and cheaply available to any and all who asked for them, there would be almost no unwanted pregnancies:

> Many of our laws on sexual conduct are a dead letter; they are not enforced and few now intend or expect them to be ... If all the laws about sex now on the books were rigorously and impartially enforced, most of the population would be in jail. (*Escape from Childhood*, p. 209)

But adults have some rights in the matter too. It seems only right and fair that as long as a young person has chosen to remain a child, dependent on his or her parents or other guardians, that person's sex life, at least in their house, should be the parents' business. If they approve of, or at least do not mind, the young person having sexual relations with others, there is no problem. But if they dislike it or disapprove of it, there is no reason why they should have to allow it to go on under their noses.

The book concludes with some suggestions about the steps to take. One way to work for a truly different and better world is to begin to act in our daily lives, as far as we can, as if that world existed. We can begin to treat children, even the youngest, wherever we may find them, as we would want everyone to treat them in the society we are trying to make. We can begin by trying to be courteous to them:

> I know very well that modern childhood is hard on adults as well as children, that it is as hard to raise a child as to be a child, and is getting harder all the time. I hope that what I propose may soon make it easier for both of them. (*Escape from Childhood*, p. 218)

Chapter 9

Instead of Education: Ways to Help People Do Things Better

John Holt begins *Instead of Education* by defining education in the way most people do, as 'something that some people do to others for their own good, moulding and shaping them, and trying to make them learn what they ought to know'. He dismissed this view of education and declared (1) that it was harmful, (2) that it could not be reformed, and (3) that it could not be carried out wisely or humanely. This was because its purpose was neither wise nor humane. The school built on this set of assumptions suffered from the three Cs of compulsion, coercion and competition, and it encouraged fear, threats, bribes and greed.

Education as imposition versus education as 'doing'

Holt's own preferred view of education was quite different, but he decided to leave the word aside altogether and talk instead of the contrasting idea of 'doing'. This word in fact restates his view of education: that it is something people get for themselves, not something to be given to them or done to them. Holt saw this as a matter of fundamental human rights:

> Next to life itself, the most fundamental of all human rights is the right to control our own minds and thoughts. That means, the right to decide for ourselves how we will explore the world around us, think about our own and other people's experiences, and find the meaning of our lives.
>
> Whoever takes that right away from us, by trying to 'educate' us, attacks the very centre of our being and does us a most profound and lasting injury. He tells us, in effect, that we cannot even be trusted to think, that for all our lives we must depend on others to tell us the meaning of our world and our lives, and that any meaning we may make for ourselves, out of our own experience, has no value. (*Instead of Education*, p. 8)

Consequently, the authoritarian school is the most dangerous of social inventions, because it sustains a modern version of slavery in which most people are shaped to be nothing more than consumers, producers, spectators and 'fans', driven by greed, envy and fear. Holt admits that he can expect to speak only to the minority of people who recognize that children, like all of us, will

> live better, learn more, and grow more able to cope with the world if they are not constantly bribed, wheedled, bullied, threatened, humiliated, and hurt; if they are not set endlessly against each other in a race which all but a few must lose; if they are not constantly made to feel incompetent, stupid, untrustworthy, guilty, fearful, and ashamed; if their interests, concerns, and enthusiasms are not ignored or scorned; and if instead they are allowed, encouraged, and (if they wish) helped to work with and help each other, to learn from each other, and to think, talk, write, and read about the things that most excite and interest them. (*Instead of Education*, p. 11)

Natural learning

Holt's basic proposition is that children do not need to be made to learn about the world because they are born as natural learners who both want to and know how to make sense of their environment. The most impressive piece of evidence on Holt's side is the fact that children teach themselves their native tongue and even coach their parents in the dovetailing skills needed to support them in this task.

The advice to parents that is derived from this analysis is stark. Do not waste energy trying to reform these schools. If you can find ways to escape schooling, do so. If not, try to find ways outside school to nourish the children's curiosity and confidence in themselves as competent learners. The bigger task in which Holt was engaged himself was to 'blow the cover' of authoritarian schooling by revealing the assortment of alibis, myths, lies and illusions.

One of these myths is that of the alleged primacy of school learning. Schools trade on the idea that 'if I want to learn anything important, I have to go to a place called school and get someone called a teacher to teach it to me; (2) the process will be boring and painful' (*Instead of Education*, p. 14).

There are few experiences from which we learn nothing, so there remains the question of what it is that we really learn from authoritarian schooling. Holt lists anger, resentment, self-contempt and self-hatred for allowing ourselves to be pushed around or used by others, for not having been smart enough or strong enough to resist or refuse. (Alice Miller goes further than Holt and adds that we learn the subconscious, festering desire to take revenge on somebody, and this usually turns out to be one's own children, who in turn are bullied into doing things 'for their own good' and sent on to authoritarian schooling in their turn.)

Natural learning is based on the idea that doing is learning. Holt explains that we learn to talk by talking and we learn to walk by walking. But our confidence in this simple principle is eroded by outside interference. Some of this interference is based on false assumptions about knowledge. What we call 'bodies of knowledge' or 'subjects' are not nouns but *verbs*. They are things people do:

> These are simply different ways in which we look at parts of the wholeness of reality and human experience and ask certain kinds of questions about them. History is the *act* of asking questions about certain aspects of the past. So are Geology and Palaeontology, but the questions are different. Physics and Chemistry are ways of asking questions about the non-living world about us. And so on. All of these are, of course, collective acts; we do them with other people, and many people have done them over the years. Thus each one of these human activities has its own history, and at least part of Mathematics or Physics or Philosophy is the account of what other mathematicians or physicists or philosophers have done. But our 'knowledge' of these things is a record of what these people *did*; what questions they asked, how they went about getting their answers, what answers they got, what conclusions they drew from their answers. (*Instead of Education*, p. 20)

Schools for 'doers'

There are examples to be found of schools that are 'doing' places. Holt gives the examples of typing schools, driving schools, dance schools, ski schools, karate schools, language schools and cooking schools. These schools differ from the compulsory, coercive child schools in various ways. People choose to go to them. It is unusual for there to be an entrance test to see whether we are smart enough to do the activity. We stay only as long as we find it helpful. Attendance is based on an agreement that if you will do certain things, the school will in turn teach you what you want to learn. Often, there is a 'no success, no charge' undertaking by the school: for example, if we do not get you through the driving test after you have followed our course, your money will be refunded. In these 'doing' schools, the teachers work to a different set of assumptions. For one thing, they accept that they are there to make themselves redundant: when the learner has passed the driving test, the teacher is no longer required.

The Beacon Hill Free School in Boston is described by Holt as an example of a school that is for 'doing'. The school has four sessions a year and each session begins with a general meeting. People come to the meeting either to offer a course or activity, or to learn what will be on offer. Anyone can offer a course, and no proof of competence is asked for. The power of the teacher to hold the class together is seen as sufficient, and the students are seen as capable of making judgments affecting their own welfare. The offers are made into a catalog. Places to meet are located in the community and may often be in the homes of the people concerned. There are no charges. The only expense of running the school is the cost of the catalog. It has no political ideology. It is just a human learning exchange. Other US cities organize something similar and call it a Learning Exchange. The one in Illinois lists 43 instruments and musical activities for those who want to develop their musical interests. The chief drawback of such learning exchanges is that success creates the problems of growth, so that a full-time secretary may be required and there can be a shortage of spaces for meeting. Although these exchanges operate for adults, the principles could be applied to children in the form of invitational schools.

The public library is another example of a 'doing' and an 'invitational' school, even though we do not call it a school. It is simply there for anyone to use if they have a need for it. The services available could easily be extended to encourage small presses:

We have learned, or been taught to think, that Freedom of the Press means the right of multimillionaire owners of newspapers or radio or TV stations to print and say whatever they like ... But this isn't what Freedom of the Press was first supposed to mean. It meant freedom to run a press, that is, to print and spread one's own ideas. (*Instead of Education*, p. 42)

Libraries could also be extended to the loan of musical instruments and could provide music practice facilities. There could also be 'tool' libraries for arts and crafts, for household repairs and for car maintenance. But then, the present school facilities could be made available on the same basis if we abandoned the idea of compulsory attendance. We would need a new kind of teacher. As well as the current 'sage on the stage', we would need 'guides on the side'. These would be learning coaches guiding the learning plans of family members in a variety of locations.

Volunteer reading guides

Holt repeats his idea, introduced in *Freedom and Beyond*, of an approach to learning to read using volunteer 'reading guides'. A public library, or a reconstructed invitational school, could be the organizational base for such a scheme:

> They would be volunteers. College or high school students or even younger children, if they could read, could be reading guides; or house-wives, or older and retired people; or librarians; or parking lot attendants; or anyone else who in his daily life might come into contact with children or other non-readers. (*Instead of Education*, p. 45)

When any guide was wearing their identifying badge, hat or armband, they could be asked one of two questions. One was 'What does this word say?'; the other was 'How do you write such and such a word?' For these tasks, no training or testing would be necessary.

Magazines are already a resource for 'doers', and Holt quotes the case of *Mother Earth News* and the development of greener and more independent lifestyles, but points out that many do-it-yourself magazines for hobbies, car repair and household repair already exist. Cooperatives for house building, food buying and other activities were other examples of 'doing' schools. The existing provision of sports facilities for anyone in the community was another resource to encourage a nation of players rather than spectators.

One development Holt admired was the Peckham Experiment in the UK, where a health and recreational facility organized as a club for families ran in London from 1935 to 1939, when the war dispersed its families and staff. Appendix B of the book is devoted to extensive quotations from this experiment because Holt was so impressed by it: 'No institution I know of expresses so well in action what I have come to believe about the needs of children and adults in society' (*Instead of Education*, p. 59).

Choosing your teacher

The next theme Holt tackles is that of the relationship between 'doers' and teachers. In many of the cases of 'doing' schools for driving, dancing, cook-ing or skiing, the learners choose the task and then enter into a voluntary agreement with a teacher, who usually breaks down the task into stages to help the learner learn the activity. If the desired learning does not result, the learner is free to choose another teacher. These 'doing' activities tend to be muscular and should not be confused with reading, which is not. Holt has already criticized as a serious mistake such a 'breaking down into skills' approach in the case of reading.

This model of teaching excludes the publishing of results for all to see unless the learner agrees to it, for the relationship is based on choice, on trust and on personally monitored feedback about whether the learning is successful. Teaching in school is not like this:

> 'A compact of trust'. Yes – but how can there be a compact of trust when the student is not free to choose what he shall learn, or when, or how, or with how much and with what kind of help? How can there be a compact of trust when the student is not free to choose or change his teacher? How can there be a compact of trust when the teacher may be obliged (as I once was), in order to keep his job, to do things he knows will harm the student, destroy his confidence and ability to learn? Or when the teacher is obliged, if the student does something poorly, to tell the whole world, to put it into a record which will follow the student all his life? (*Instead of Education*, p. 63)

In Holt's preferred model of teaching, the key task is for teachers to help the students become independent and to learn to be their own teachers. True teachers must always be trying to work themselves out of a job.

Learner-managed learning and the question of standards

One of Holt's fellow musicians, on hearing that he was teaching himself the cello, asked him about standards. Where did they come from if he did not have a teacher? Holt replies that they came from the top cellists whose playing he heard on recordings or at concerts. Standards exist in the public domain and are not kept enshrined in compulsory schools. In many cases, feedback on performance and standards can be compared by using video or other types of recordings, and this is used widely in the learning of sports.

Dismissing your teacher

Teachers can easily get in the way of learning, especially if they fall in love with a particular sequence of tasks and try to fit all the learners into it. This is a common problem with school subject teachers, especially as most school subjects are not sequential at all. In 'doing' schools this is resolved by the student choosing another teacher – a solution rarely on offer in compulsory schooling.

Holt draws on his experience in the Ny Lilleskole in Copenhagen, where the model of teaching had many of the features he admired. Children learned reading, rather than the teachers teaching it. The teachers operated like the 'reading guides' mentioned earlier, by being available to help on request. The usual kind of testing has no place in this approach. The only kind of testing is the kind the learner needs to 'locate their place on the map':

> Maps put up to help strangers get around in cities have on them an arrow and the words 'You are here'. Without that, the maps are useless. This is the only legitimate use of tests – to find out where a student is, so that the teacher may better order his tasks, or help him explore. (*Instead of Education*, p. 83)

Other kinds of tests just induce students to start figuring out what the tester wants, not what the learners need. Their purpose is to grade, rank and label learners, not to help them.

Teaching questions, not answers

It is relatively easy to teach people to give right answers but much harder to teach them how to ask the right questions, questions that are interesting, important, useful and far-reaching. All existing knowledge began with someone asking questions, and the subjects are records of the answers to date. Thus, history is not a set of facts but a collection of reports, often about as reliable as the reports in a typical newspaper. Holt links this idea to a proposition for a new kind of teacher, rather like the reading guides described earlier: 'No question, no teaching' (*Instead of Education*, p. 87).

Even then, teachers cannot give knowledge: an answer to a question is an attempt to put part of the teacher's experience into words, so the receiver gets the words but not the experience. To make meaning and form knowledge, the receiver must use their own experience. The teacher can only try to connect their experience with that of the enquirer.

Schoolbooks are misleading, for they usually record the answers but not the process of finding out. A useful type of book, Holt suggests, would show the mistakes researchers made and the experiments that led nowhere. They could also show how the experts disagree. Such books would help readers to learn how to set about asking appropriate questions.

Natural authority versus official authority

Following the idea of George Dennison in *Lives of Children* (New York: Random House, 1969), Holt draws a clear distinction between two versions of authority, as he did in *Freedom and Beyond*. Natural authority is based on wisdom, competence, experience and commitment, whereas official authority is based on coercion and the power to bribe, threaten and punish. The latter undermines and destroys the former. Power removes moral obligations: slaves have no moral duty to obey orders and every moral right to avoid them if they can. Under the official authority regime, the student has unlimited obligations to the school sustained by coercive power.

Under a natural authority approach, no one could be another person's teacher unless both parties freely agreed to the arrangement. In a situation where people had learned to teach themselves, such arrangements would be found, but less frequently than under official authority systems. A teacher–student relationship is a superior–inferior situation, so both parties should clearly understand the nature of such a contract, and its length, purposes and duration. School is set up on the basis of official authority and not natural authority. It is a compulsory treatment place where one group of people called 'teachers' do all sorts of things to another called 'students', whether the students want them to or not. The arguments as to why this is supposed to be necessary are dubious. Holt cites the example of officials who pronounce that no one has the right to be illiterate. Yet at any time I choose to visit a foreign country, I claim precisely such a right. Few tourists would pass any basic literacy test in the language of the countries they visit.

Views of human nature

The common view of human nature is pessimistic and is derived from religion. It proposes that people who are free, will end up doing wrong. The few people who can be trusted, therefore, need to take charge and impose a social order and change it as little as possible. This view is called conservative, or reactionary, or fascist, according to the degree of coercion invoked. Holt sees himself as a conservative who does not hold the pessimistic view:

> Though I am in many ways conservative, finding it better to conserve than waste or destroy, I do not think that in order to be a true conservative one must take the traditional and dark view that humans are naturally bad. (*Instead of Education*, p. 116)

Although humans have done many bad things, he argues, there are also plenty of examples of the good. We focus on the bad partly because it is easier to do so, easier to destroy than create, and partly because it makes more of an impression – it is 'news'. What is true, therefore, is that humans are very malleable and can be shaped by culture into people who mostly behave badly, or into people who mostly behave well. The political theory derived from the pessimistic conservative view has a poor track record:

> The bad is most likely to rise to the top . . . Much of what we call History is the success stories of madmen. How many times, on their various roads to glory, power, empire, etc., must these men and their armies of thugs and killers have wiped out societies far more sensible and humane. (*Instead of Education*, p. 118)

The 'survival of the fittest' theory, dear to those who hold the pessimistic conservative view, really means the 'survival of the morally least fit'. Holt proposes that people do bad things because they have learned to do so from their society and not because of any notion of Original Sin:

> People do many of the bad things, even the worst things, they do because they are taught and made to do them. Perhaps the society they live in tells them, as ours tells us, that since winning is the only thing, it is good to be greedy, selfish, ruthless, hard-nosed, and tough. (*Instead of Education*, p. 119)

There is no way to find out how much good and kindness there is in human nature except by building a society on the assumption that people are, or would like to be, good and kind, where being good and kind is not a handicap. Holt returns to the country that records the highest score on the International Index of Social Progress: Denmark. (Neither the USA nor the UK appears in the top ten of this index. The UK did score 13th out of 124 nations in the late 1980s but is reported to have dropped several places since and may now be occupying about 20th place.) The Ny Lilleskole in Copenhagen is a school Holt sees as trying to implement the more positive view of human nature:

> In fact it is a 'doing' place. In it about eighty-five children, aged six or seven to about fourteen, come together with a group of six adults, who work with the children to make a community which is lively, interesting, pleasant, secure, trusting, co-operative and humane. (*Instead of Education*, p. 121)

The school is quite different from the usual US school and different from the so-called 'open' British primary school, which Holt sees as just another, albeit softer, version of an authoritarian adult-directed school: 'There are no subjects, no courses, no classes, no pre-planned paths down which the children progress at their own rate, no texts or exams, no marks or grades or report cards, no reports of any kind' (*Instead of Education*, p. 122).

Holt notes that he had to see a place like this to have any idea of what it is like to trust children to find out about the world and what happens when you do. The reason is that we are so used to the game that adults and children play in the usual place called school that our imagination freezes. Having seen Ny Lilleskole, he reports that he could hardly stand to visit most schools anymore, even schools that a few year earlier he might have seen as good. Although most Danes do not send their children to such a school, the approach developed there has influenced the other schools in Denmark. Furthermore, this will continue, because the 'Schools of the Future' project of 1990–3 drew many of its recommendations from such examples. Holt devotes several pages to describing the school, and there is no substitute for consulting the original text at this point and reading about why he was so impressed.

The teachers at the school have natural authority because they are intelligent, informed, interested and interesting. They know a lot about the world and they think about it. They are not alienated. They do not hate their lives or despise their country or hate the world, although they want to try to improve it. They like being grown-up and have a zest for life.

Holt contrasts this with his experience of US teachers and with surveys of teachers in mainstream schools which show that they read very little – about one new book per year – and are not very well informed or curious to find out things:

> Like average people in most modern countries, they don't know much and they can't do much – and what they know or can do, they don't talk about or do in school. In short, they are not people that curious, active, and healthy children would choose to spend much time with. (*Instead of Education*, p. 134)

The repeated failure of school reform

As the movement to reform US schools grinds to a halt, John Holt points out that this has happened before. It happened in the 1920s and 1930s. The approaches seen as 'revolutionary' were to be found in the schools of Indiana in 1905. Earlier still, in 1875, Colonel Parker began work in the schools of Quincy, Massachusetts, drawing on ideas gained after several years' study in Europe:

> Parker began his work of educational reconstruction by tearing out the network of partitions and passageways represented by the traditional school subjects. He abolished reading, spelling, arithmetic, geography,

etc., as separate school subjects and had them reappear as useful accomplishments and interesting aspects of an experience which was a united, interrelated whole. On the side of discipline, he abolished rules, prizes, demerits, marks, and the entire repressive apparatus which bribed or threatened children into being industrious or orderly. In place of this repressive system of school control, he worked with his teachers to build up a real sense of community in which people learned to conduct themselves as thoughtful, co-operative, public-spirited citizens. (*Instead of Education*, p. 142)

These reforms never last long. They fall out of fashion, reaction sets in and the schools that have tried to be more humane give up, one by one. The public heaves a sigh of relief, and all the accumulated long-term failings that set the reforms going in the first place are now blamed on the few reform efforts and the reformers. Evidence is studiously ignored in this process. Thus, the study by the Carnegie Foundation in the 1930s, which showed that, on all counts, open, flexible, interest-oriented approaches led to better results than formal instruction and rote memorization, was instantly forgotten.

The first myth that Holt points to is that there has ever been very much of the more successful approach actually to be found anywhere. Ten per cent or less of the whole child population has ever been involved at any one time. Most of the schools involved have been small. The amount of money spent on them has been small. The return of the pressure for formal grades was inevitable because even if schools changed, colleges and universities would not, and this always effectively sabotaged change. At the height of the so-called happy and permissive years in schools, Charles Silberman and a large team of researchers reported on US schools and, funded by the Carnegie Trust, gave their findings in a book originally entitled 'Murder in the Classroom' but actually issued under the title of *Crisis in the Classroom* in 1970 after protests:

It is not possible to spend any prolonged period visiting public school classrooms without being appalled by the mutilation visible everywhere – mutilation of spontaneity, of joy in learning, or pleasure in creating, or sense of self ... Because adults take the schools so much for granted, they fail to appreciate what grim, joyless places most American schools are, how oppressive and petty are the rules by which they are governed, how intellectually sterile and aesthetically barren the atmosphere, what an appalling lack of civility obtains on the part of teachers. (*Crisis in the Classroom*, p. 146)

A great deal of the so-called reform, Holt observes, never got past the stage of window dressing, conferences and empty talk. In Vermont, the State Department put out a document, 'The Vermont Idea in Education', which was a radical declaration about changing schools. A few years later, a Vermont teacher confided to Holt that nobody in the state took it seriously and only about three schools ever made any serious efforts to implement it.

This is not about personal cruelty by teachers, Holt explains. Compulsory and competitive schools are cruel by their very nature. Even if physical cruelty reduces, mental cruelty increases as more and more of children's time and attention is taken up by school requirements. Holt describes a kindergarten report card made up of 62 items. The children were checked and graded on these items. After only eight weeks a teacher was confidently informing a father that his child would never be a scholar, on the basis of the checklist results.

The 'back to the basics' movement in the USA was based on a myth: that schools in general had ever moved away from them, although their attempts had met with variable success. A more accurate slogan would have been 'do the basics better'. The school Holt worked in had never moved away from the formal teaching of the basics using strict, old-fashioned methods in a rich neighborhood of well-motivated families. It was observing the poor results of this experience that led Holt to research and then write *How Children Fail* and start his search for something more effective.

One reason few schools had changed is that, from the point of view of most people, they were not failing in the tasks people required of them. Holt quotes one teacher who after 30 years of attending conferences, training sessions and workshops remarked that after each one they just returned to reality and carried on more or less as before: 'which was to try to bribe, scare, and shame children into learning what someone else had decided they ought to know' (*Instead of Education*, p. 160).

Therefore, schools were actually doing what most people wanted, although what people wanted was not the providing of education, but the setting of a series of social tasks for the convenience of adults. They included the following:

To shut young people out of adult society

In modern societies, children are a problem. Nobody wants them around. Mothers are usually tired of having them around the house. Shopkeepers do not want them on the streets. Workers do not want them in workplaces. Nobody has any use for them. Schools provide an answer to this problem.

To sort children into winners and losers

Most modern societies are organized into winners and losers, and the grading, labeling, marking and examining activity of schools does the preliminary work, not only by doing the ranking but by persuading the losers that this is fair. They deserve to be losers since they had their chance. That the rich children were bound to win in a rigged contest is undeclared.

For all the talk about wanting all children to succeed, most parents want school to get their children ahead of the others and make them winners. If teachers took the rhetoric seriously and organized learning so well that all got top marks, they would soon be accused of soft marking and be subject to investigation for sabotaging the grading system. Schools cannot afford to ape the car-driving test philosophy and methodology, where everyone is expected to pass, and almost everyone does:

> They cannot afford to give all good grades, to say that all of their students are winners. They are, after all, selling tickets to jobs and careers. The more good grades they give, the less their tickets are worth. The 'best' colleges and universities are those that can say that their standards are so high that almost no students are good enough to meet them. (*Instead of Education*, p. 165)

Schools may pretend that they want equal opportunities for rich and poor children alike but the reality is different. The stuff schools teach is closer to the lives of the better-off children. The language used is Standard English – the way rich people talk. The task for the poor child is many times more difficult:

> A really poor child, to become a winner ... must somehow dodge the low tracks, escape or ignore the prejudice and contempt of his teachers, meet the risks of learning without emotional support, face increasing hostility from his loser friends, and find meaning in instructional materials which have little or nothing to do with his life or experience. Above all, in spite of never hearing it outside of school, and barely being allowed to talk in school at all, he must learnt to talk middle-class English. (*Instead of Education*, p. 167)

As long as we care more about the growth of industrial output than we do about the happiness and growth of people, Holt comments, this state of affairs will continue.

There are consolation prizes on offer which less ambitious parents value. If your child is not a winner, then at least there is the possibility of becoming a loser rather than a bad loser. Losers can expect mundane work, part-time work and a low standard of living. Bad losers end up as drunks, drug addicts or in jail. Teachers are given license to impose, sooner or later, whatever is necessary to try to prevent this.

Holt introduces one of the best short analyses of the hidden curriculum to be found. He describes four sets of ideas children learn in schools, the official curriculum and three types of unwritten curriculum:

> Liberal and radical critics of the schools have long charged, I think with good reason, that on the whole they teach contempt for non-white people, women, manual workers, and the poor; a narrow and uncritical, and belligerent patriotism; too great respect for wealth and power; and a love of toughness, competition, struggle, and violence. (*Instead of Education*, p. 175)

Teachers could work to change all of these if they wanted to, but choose not to because most of them share the attitudes of the society around them. Schools, however, can carry multiple and contradictory messages, so that other critics say that schools teach immorality, atheistic science and socialism or worse.

The fifth set of ideas learned in schools are outside the power of teachers to change. This is the power to make school compulsory, for most children, with the procedures of ranking and labeling. Along with this go the messages of implicit distrust and contempt:

> If we didn't make you come here you wouldn't learn anything, you'd just waste your time ... Even if you could be trusted to want to find out about the world, you are too stupid to do it. Not only do we have to decide what you need to learn, but then we have to show you, one tiny step at a time, how to learn it. You could never figure it out for yourself, or even have enough sense to ask good questions about it. The world is too complicated, mysterious, and difficult for you. We can't let you explore it. We must make sense of it for you. You can only learn from us. (*Instead of Education*, p. 175)

The enduring message is that if you want to learn something of importance, it can be done only in a school from a teacher. It is belief in the Divine Right of Experts.

The aim is for children to learn how to become the same as their parents, who have learned to live mostly by fear and greed. Despite sporadic talk about sharing and cooperation, the serious business is spelled out: it is gaining advantages over other people starting by doing better in the school tests:

They teach that the serious work of making sense of the world cannot be done co-operatively, but must be done in a dog-eat-dog competition. They teach that greed is not a vice to be mastered but a virtue to be encouraged. And, like all situations that make winning all-important, they teach cheating. (*Instead of Education*, p. 179)

For those who ask what the evidence is that people really slavishly obey authority as a result, among other influences, of their schooling, John Holt turns to some of the most chilling, unpopular, suppressed and hastily forgotten research. It is the research of Stanley Milgram published in his book *Obedience to Authority: An Experimental View* in 1974. In opposition to the claim that schools are teaching morality, responsibility and all the social and civic virtues, Holt looks at Milgam's findings. His chapter 15, 'The Obedient Torturers', is devoted to an account of Milgram's experiments, and for those not familiar with the work it needs to be consulted.

In brief, Milgram showed how ordinary US citizens would, under the instructions of authority, give other citizens, whom they had never met, electric shocks past the points of danger. Psychologists had estimated that only 1 per cent or less of people – those who were very mentally sick – would do this. The results were different. Over 60 per cent of men and women in the samples, in various US cities, were willing to go to the end of the pain scale. Holt concludes that it would not be difficult to recruit guards for Nazi-style concentration camps in the USA (or the UK for that matter), as Milgram's research shows. People asked to explain their behavior afterwards gave the standard response of the Nazis that they were only obeying orders. In response to questions about how they would feel if the person they gave shocks to died, Milgram records answers like this: 'So he's dead. I did my job!' Morality has now been changed from this person's views of right and wrong, to a concern for how well he is living up to the expectations of authority. Holt links this directly with the messages of compulsory schooling:

They teach people to obey authority, i.e. to push the 450-volt button on command. But of course a compulsory and coercive institution could not do anything else, even if it wanted to. School people talk all the time about 'teaching responsibility'. Yet it is absurd to think that an institution that commands and judges every part of a child's life and thought can make him more responsible. It can only make him less so. (*Instead of Education*, p. 189)

Holt cites the research of Lawrence Kohlberg to show that morality develops only when people have the opportunity to exercise their capacities for moral judgment. But where in school are people ever given such opportunities?

To talk of using the schools to teach morality is a bad joke. We might as well talk of using the Army to teach pacifism. As Edgar Friedenberg has well put it, powerlessness corrupts. The schools, by taking the power to make choices from their students, corrupt them. (*Instead of Education*, p. 191)

Lest there be any confusion, Holt returns to an earlier point that official authority and natural authority are different. Milgram's research was about the former and not the latter.

Holt concludes that schools based on the current model are, therefore, bad places because they have bad tasks. Many do not see this. There are five groups of people that can be identified. Some believe that schools are all right but need to be stricter and more conventional. Others believe that they are all right but need more resources and better techniques. There are those who think they are all right but need to treat poor and black children better. 'Progressive' reformers think they are all right but need to treat all children in more humane ways.

Holt sees himself as a member of a fifth group, those who see schools as having bad purposes which require radical changes. The objection Holt has to them is not, as with the first four groups, technical but *moral*. To reform them we will need to change their purposes: 'They must not be jails for the young ... they must not be allowed to rank and label their students' (*Instead of Education*, p. 195). The near-monopoly of school over credentials would have to be broken in the process, otherwise making schools invitational would be a futile gesture. Children would still have to go to get the certificates.

When schools become invitational, they also become more flexible. Students could choose different learning experiences in different schools. Off-site neighborhood tutorial groups could be set up, as well as local learning exchanges.

Teachers and reform

When John Holt began teaching, he simply wanted some interesting and pleasant work to do. He did not see himself as trying to make a better society or finding truth, or reforming education: 'I had no quarrel with traditional education. If someone had said to me much of what I have said in this book, my answer would have been, "Balony!" I agreed without question that students should be made to learn' (*Instead of Education*, p. 207). Most of his ideas about education came out of the concrete realities of solving the problems of how he could get this child to learn to read, to spell or to solve this or that problem. He came to realize that to teach in a school was about as subversive as working for General Motors or the Pentagon. Teachers who see themselves as radical rarely change anything, he concluded, and they become frustrated by their failures to teach children to think. They are fooling themselves because they are themselves coerced into doing the business of the school. It is like a soldier claiming to be a pacifist crying, 'I hate war! All men are brothers! Thou shalt not kill!' as he shoots at the enemy.

He wrote to one young teacher who was asking how he could change the schools:

> You are going to have your hands full, just trying to find or make for yourself a spot in which you can do not too much harm, be reasonably honest with your students, help some of them cope a little better with the problems of school, and get some fun out of your work. To do even that little will not be easy. (*Instead of Education*, p. 209)

A winner–loser society is not going to be changed by the winners, and as long as schools remain compulsory, coercive and competitive, any changes will be short-lived, or not go very deep, or not spread very far.

Do we have a chance?

Holt concludes by suggesting what parents can do about schooling. They can, indeed, campaign to do away with them: 'Schools are not a force of nature. People made them, thinking they would be useful; people can do away with them when they are no longer of any use' (*Instead of Education*, p. 213).

When more parents ask questions about why all adults should be taxed to provide a system of schools from which the children of the rich and affluent gain the most, and what *kind* of schools we are running where the poor children always seem to lose out, reform can become possible.

In the meantime, Holt can think of only three options open to parents:

1. Help your children cope with school as it is.
2. Help your children to escape.
3. Give them an alternative.

These options can be used together to achieve damage limitation:

> All the children I have known who were coping best with school, doing well at it, and more or less happy in it, led the largest and most interesting

and important parts of their lives outside of school. Children who do not like school and are not doing well there, but cannot escape it, need such an out-of-school life even more. And children who escape school must have some alternative, some interesting and pleasant (to them) way of spending the time that other children spend in school. (*Instead of Education*, p. 215)

In addition, the hidden curriculum of the school is best exposed by being honest with children about these matters and expressing healthier values in their life and work. The request of schools to back them up and say that 'if pupils get into trouble at school they can expect to get into more trouble at home', should be treated with scepticism. Often the best thing is to do nothing dramatic, but listen to children sympathetically, because often what a child needs most is what school is denying them: a chance to tell their story to people who will listen and try to understand. This action by parents shows that they take the child's feelings seriously, and this alone may be enough to help their children make the best of it.

If a parent is impelled to write to the school, Holt suggests something short and constructive in these tones: 'My child says this happened. I don't know whether it did or not. I hope it did not, but if it did, please don't let it happen again' (*Instead of Education*, p. 217).

Apart from that, parents can help by showing their children some of the tricks that will help them play the school game better. The children can be helped to realize that the school game is as unreal and abstract as chess, but beating it requires the learning of the tricks. Useless though most of it is, there are the rewards for playing it well, those of the college entrance and the job tickets. Some of Holt's own books are full of such ideas, for example *What Do I do Monday?* and *How Children Learn* and *Learning All the Time*. One tip is to buy the books used in school, and especially the teacher's manual, for use both by the parents and the children.

The option of escape and providing the one alternative of home-based education is, of course, the subject of one of Holt's books, *Teach Your Own*. Starting a small school or, alternatively, organizing a group of home-educating families in a cooperative learning scheme, is another possibility. Holt speculates that children learning out of school are likely to learn much faster and better than children in school. The evidence of home-based effectiveness research is now available to show that he was right: they are, on average, two years ahead of their schooled peers, and the gap appears to have been widening. Holt ends this book in uncompromising fashion: 'Meanwhile, education – compulsory schooling, compulsory learning – is a tyranny and a crime against the human mind and spirit. Let all those escape it who can, any way they can' (*Instead of Education*, p. 226).

Chapter 10

Never Too Late

As was noted earlier, when I met John Holt at the railway station in Birmingham in 1982, he arrived complete with his cello. This somewhat unusual piece of luggage was an indication of the priority he gave to his music in the later years of his life. In between his speaking engagements he would return to our house and settle down to play.

Never Too Late: My Musical Life Story is the most autobiographical of Holt's books, and although it is mostly the story of his love affair with music, strands of information about other aspects of his life are woven into it. He tells us that he came from an almost nonmusical family and therefore did not learn to play an instrument as a child. He had no burning regrets about this, for he noted how plenty of people he met who had been compelled to learn an instrument in their youth had had their love of music diminished and sometimes extinguished in the process.

He began to play the flute at the age of 34. He switched to the cello at 40 and played for two years. Few adults who have never played take up an instrument in middle age, and least of all a bowed string instrument, since string instruments are supposed to be the hardest to learn. At the age of 50, he took up the cello again and also began to write up his experiences in the hope that his story might encourage other people, above all adults, who may have been told that they were too old to begin to play a musical instrument. By now, he saw the task of becoming a skillful musician as the most important remaining task of his life.

This book that recorded his experiences of becoming a musician was also another of his works about education, about teaching, especially self-teaching and also learning, especially learner-managed learning:

This is also a book about teaching, above all the teaching of music. Some music teachers have been enormously helpful to me ... But for the most part I am self-taught in music, and this book is also about that self-teaching. Part of the art of learning any difficult act, like music, is knowing both how to teach yourself and how best to use the teaching of others, how to gain from the greater experience and skill of other people without becoming dependent on them. (*Never Too Late*, p. 2)

Holt finishes this passage with the memorable observation that 'What we can best learn from good teachers is how to teach ourselves better.'

Holt adopted this as his definition of good teaching. Inadequate teachers work *on* children, keeping them dependent, whereas good teachers work *with* children, encouraging them to teach themselves and become independent. Self-teaching involves a series of stages: trial and error, feedback, self-correction, satisfaction, and pleasure when it is a success. *Never Too Late* had a central concern with exploration and discovery.

A few general pieces of information about his life appear throughout the book. As we saw in Chapter 2, his parents were quite well-off, so he had an easy and comfortable young life. As an adult, he chose to live with very little money so that he could do work he believed in, initially in the peace movement. He managed to maintain his modest lifestyle without many worries about money. The fact that he did not marry was a contributory factor.

But he had sufficient money to be able to explore, enjoy and make music. *Never Too Late* was, in part, an attack on fatalism, for he questioned the belief that what happens to us in the first few years of life determines what follows. He proposed instead that it is never too late, a message that has cheered many an adult since.

Another task Holt set himself was to question a commonly held belief that becoming a competent musician requires relentless external compulsion. This was an erroneous and dangerous doctrine. Moreover, he denied that the task of becoming musical required forced exposure, coercion and threat. He set out to combat the idea that any disciplined activity, such as making music, can never grow out of love, joy and free choice.

Most of what was written about musical education said, in one way or another, that children needed to be compelled to become musical. Holt declared that this idea is not only mistaken but dangerous; nothing is more likely to make most people ignore or even hate great music than trying to ram more and more of it down the throats of more and more children in compulsory classes and lessons:

The idea is wrong in a larger sense; in the long run, love and joy are more enduring sources of discipline and commitment than any amount of bribe and threat, and it is only what C. Wright Mills called the 'crackpot realism' of our times that keeps us from seeing, or even being willing to see, that this is so. (*Never Too Late*, p. 5)

Never Too Late is the most personal of Holt's books, for it contains many detailed anecdotes concerning his life and his musical life in particular. We learn that John Holt went away to school at Exeter, New Hampshire, and discovered the big band sound of Tommy Dorsey. He also joined the school glee club. Later, he developed an interest in classical music. His musical autobiography develops in chapters headed 'Stravinsky and Woody Herman' and 'I Meet Beethoven'.

There was not too much music around in his family. Only one family member, his Aunt Jessie, could play an instrument, the piano, so when she was around, evenings could be given over to singing the songs that his aunt played on the large black upright piano at his grandmother's house.

College set back his musical development, when he applied to join the Freshman Glee Club. He was rejected because his voice was deemed 'foggy, throaty and wheezy':

> But it still makes me regretful, and angry, that when I found out, almost by accident, that I loved making music and wanted more than anything to make some more, a rich university, dedicated (so they say) to the higher things of life, could have found nothing better to do than to slam the door in my face. (*Never Too Late*, pp. 65–6)

Later, he and some friends formed a barbershop quartet. The quartet enjoyed a short life, singing together and performing at parties, until a key member moved on to get married. After that, Holt purchased a guitar and it gave him great pleasure for several years. But when he began teaching, he had little spare time for playing and so gave the guitar to one of his nephews.

He spent some time in the navy before working full-time at the New York office of World Federation, an organization promoting world government.

Then in 1952, he spent some time in England, returning to the USA in 1953 to begin teaching in Colorado, where he stayed for four years. His next move was to Boston, where he lived out the rest of his life teaching, lecturing and writing. His move there was a matter of chance. A friend and his wife offered him use of an apartment for two years while they were away in Africa. Holt took up the offer and found Boston to his liking and settled there. It was during his years in Boston that he took up the cello.

But the success of his first book, *How Children Fail*, led to invitations to lecture, and he also set to work on his second book. The cello was squeezed out of his life for a time.

As we have seen, Holt was influenced by Ivan Illich's ideas on deinstitutionalization. Holt favored deinstitutionalization and set about supporting the idea that people could act directly and cooperatively to satisfy their needs. Learning the cello now seemed an integral part of that concern, so he began again in 1973:

> If I could learn to play the cello well, as I thought I could, I could show by my own example that we all have greater powers than we think, that whatever we want to learn or learn to do, we probably can learn, that our lives and possibilities are not determined and fixed by what happened to us when we were little, or what experts say we can and cannot do. In my work with the cello, I might also find out things about learning music that might help many other adults learn it, or whatever else they wanted to learn. In short, my love for music now seemed joined to my love of teaching and to my deepest political concerns. The gap I had felt between my work and my hobby had disappeared. (*Never Too Late*, pp. 185–6)

In his reflections on his own learning of the cello, many of Holt's ideas about effective learning are reinforced. The trouble with most teachers, whether of music or anything else, is that they act on the false assumption that learning is the result of teaching, and even, in many cases, that learning *can only* be the result of teaching. Consequently, there is often an angry reaction to the idea that students might find out for themselves and an even angrier reaction to the idea that they would be better off by so doing. It is not enough for them to be helpful and useful to their students; they need to feel that their students could not get along without them:

> All my own work as a teacher and learner has led me to believe quite the opposite, that teaching is a very strong medicine, which like all strong medicines can quickly and easily turn into a poison. At the right time (i.e. when the student has asked for it) and in very small doses, it can indeed help learning. But at the wrong times, or in too large doses, it will slow down learning or prevent it altogether. (*Never Too Late*, p. 209)

Fellow musicians had also absorbed the myth, for when they asked him who his cello teacher was and he replied that he was teaching himself for the time being, they were surprised, or indignant, or even angry. It follows that Holt's definition of a good teacher will continue to surprise, cause indignation or even anger:

> The teacher I need must accept that he or she is my partner and helper and not my boss, that in this journey of musical exploration and adventure, I am the captain. Expert guides and pilots I can use, no doubt about it. But it is my expedition, I gain the most if it succeeds and lose the most if it fails, and I must remain in charge. (*Never Too Late*, p. 217)

People who learned of Holt's love of music sometimes asked him if he regretted that his parents had not made him have music lessons. His answer was negative; such forced exposure would probably have killed off his interest, as it had done for many in the past.

At this time, 1973, John Holt was also working on his book *Instead of Education*. But his work on the cello was no longer neglected. He applied the advice of Matthew Arnold to 'clear a space'. In other words, he stopped doing some things that he enjoyed in order to give time to his music. These included sailing, swimming, camping, mountain backpacking, skiing, squash, tennis, and soccer. He reports no regrets, for he saw music as being akin to athletics, as a sport more difficult and fascinating than any other he had ever played. There was as much teamwork and split-second timing in playing in an orchestra as in any sport. It was also a limitless field for thought, invention and experiment.

He also reduced his general reading. The huge stacks of magazines and books he had always read were drastically reduced in number, for he already had considerable understanding. In any case, he noted that he had already had all the bad news he could stand.

Holt received considerable encouragement as a result of meeting Janos Starker, one of the world's greatest cellists. Some friends who lived in Seattle invited him to visit when Starker was playing in a concert. When Holt arrived in Seattle, he found that a small party had been arranged with Starker in attendance. At the party, he decided to keep a low profile, but Starker approached him, saying, 'Good evening, Mr Holt.' In the conversation that followed, Holt mentioned his desire to take up the cello again. Janos Starker observed, 'Well. It's extremely difficult for someone of our age to learn to play this instrument well, because we have to develop a whole new set of muscles, and a whole new set of coordinations. On the other hand, we have an advantage.' Holt asked him to explain. 'We can think up problems, and find solutions.' This resonated with John Holt. If you want to do it, you can do it, he concluded, and it *is* possible for an old dog to learn new tricks.

Holt's general concerns for education began about this time to take a different form. He changed emphasis from giving his time to trying to improve schools to supporting home-based education:

For many years, with many others, I tried to make schools more kindly, interesting, competent, and serious. It now seems clear that in the near future this will not happen, mostly because there are so few people, in or out of schools, who want it to happen. To those few people who can't stand what schools are doing to their children, I now urge that they look for ways to take their children out altogether and have them learn at home. To help them do this I have begun to publish a newsletter, *Growing Without Schooling*. (*Never Too Late*, p. 240)

It is fitting that Holt's book should have received enthusiastic support from Sir Yehudi Menuhin since Menuhin had been educated at home. Menuhin attended school for just half a day. In a radio interview in July 1996 he explained:

Questioner: You never went to school? Or you did for one day?
Yehudi Menuhin: Not even one day; one morning. When I came back from the morning, my mother asked me what had I learnt. I said 'I really didn't learn anything. I sat at the back of the class, and there was a little window high up on the wall through which I could see branches. I hoped that a bird would alight. No bird alighted, but I kept hoping.' And that's about all I could report. So my mother promptly said, 'Well, we'll educate you at home.'

Menuhin wrote:

Never Too Late is an altogether sympathetic, heart-warming book. John Holt has found the secret of youth, for his discovery that constant studying, thinking and trying, spell constant progress, constant growth and improvement, and are, in fact, the attributes of youth.

Of course, he loved music for a considerable time and kept alive his capacity and enthusiasm for and his attention to sounds and their creation.

I applaud this book heartily; may everyone reading it stay young, well and warm-hearted in the same way. (From Menuhin's foreword to the British edition of *Never Too Late*)

But Holt's work and development as a musician continued up until his death, and, as was mentioned in Chapter 2, he became proficient enough to play in local chamber orchestras. He was not conscious of having encountered any limitations because of his late start in music. He remained convinced from his own experience that it is 'never too late': 'If Nature has waiting for me up the road some kind of impassable barrier, she has so far given me no clear signs of it' (*Never Too Late*, p. 242).

Chapter 11

Teach Your Own

Teach Your Own was published in 1981. In it John Holt set himself three tasks. First, he wanted to set out the case for home-based education. Next, he set out to report on the wealth of experience of those who were taking this path. Finally, he intended the book to be a manual for action and inspiration for those just setting out.

The book marks a significant change in Holt's thinking about education. With the success of his first two books, *How Children Fail* and *How Children Learn*, he had found himself busy as a lecturer in the USA and overseas, on the theme of making schools into places where children would be independent and self-directing learners. In this respect, *Teach Your Own* was somewhat misleading as a title since Holt had dismissed most teaching as anti-educational. But this book was meant for parents, and in any case he had allowed two exceptions in the case of teaching. One was teaching that taught you how to become a better self-teacher, and the other was invited teaching.

For a while, he and his allies assumed that changes towards self-directed teaching might well take place in many schools, and in time in most schools. By 1968, however, John Holt had begun to confront the issue of compulsion. He came to feel strongly that the kinds of changes he wanted to see in schools, starting with the ways teachers related to students, could not happen as long as schools were compulsory. Since compulsory school attendance laws forced teachers to do the work of policing conscripted learners, they were prevented from doing real teaching. It would be in the best interests of teachers, as well as those of parents and children, to have these laws repealed, and for schools to become invitational. Schools needed to become less like day prisons and more like public libraries.

Yet even as he and others lobbied for reforms along these lines in the USA, the situation began to change. For a while, he noted, school reform was in fashion, but then it went out of fashion. Holt confessed that he had not learned that in today's mass media world, ideas go in and out of fashion as quickly as clothes.

Facing up to the regressives in the USA

Regressive America began to reassert itself. Indeed, he concluded that regressive attitudes might even make up the majority view: 'Very few people, inside the schools or out, were willing to support or even tolerate giving more freedom, choice and self-direction to children' (*Teach Your Own*, p. 4).

He saw that freedom had been treated not as a serious proposition but as a trick, a motivational device. When the trick did not bring quick results, it was soon abandoned. This led him to write two books, *Escape from Childhood* and *Instead of Education*, in which he explored the uncomfortable idea that most adults in the USA actively distrust and rather dislike most children, sometimes even their own. He proposed that people whose lives are hard or boring or painful or meaningless – people who suffer – tend to resent those who seem to suffer less than they do, and will make them suffer if they can. People in chains with no apparent hope of losing them want to put chains on others:

> In short, it was becoming clear to me that the great majority of boring, regimented schools were doing exactly what most people wanted them to do. Teach children about Reality. Teach them that Life Is No Picnic. Teach them to Shut Up And Do What You're Told. (*Teach Your Own*, p. 4)

John Holt was not impressed by such schools. He said of them that they demonstrated that a school based on such a view was not just a good idea gone wrong, but a bad idea from the start. He concluded that 'Back to the Basics' was really code for 'No More Fun and Games in School'. Most adults in the USA, he observed, do not care all that much about reading, since they read little themselves. Like most Americans, young or old, they spend much of their leisure time watching TV. What they want their children to learn is how to *work*. By that they do not mean to do good and skillful work they can be proud of. They do not have that kind of work themselves, and never expect to. They do not even call that 'work'. They want their children, when their time comes, to be able and willing to hold down full-time *painful jobs* of their own. The best way to get them ready to do this is to make school as much like a full-time painful job as possible.

This was not just a working-class attitude, he noted. A middle-class couple who had transferred their son to the school Holt was teaching in were pleased that there had been a great improvement in both their son's studies and his behaviour, but expressed their anxieties thus:

'You know, his father and I worry a little about how much fun he is having in school. After all, he is going to have to spend the rest of his life doing things he doesn't like, and he may as well get used to it now.' (*Teach Your Own*, p. 8)

The reasons for these bleak attitudes were not cruelty or mean-spiritedness, but *fatalism*. In their view, this was how the world was, and it was not going to change for the better. In addition, such people had developed faith in violence as a way to solve problems, despite the evidence of its failure. While such parents were in a majority, John Holt concluded, any general movement for school reform was doomed.

There had been some early signs. In one large meeting the friendly reception for Holt's ideas was suddenly shattered by someone asking in a harsh and angry voice, 'What do you do with the children who are just plain lazy?' The entire audience burst into loud applause. The silent majority had spoken and expressed its view that children were just no good, were not to be trusted and needed compulsion.

Holt saw the effect of compulsory schooling on teachers as demeaning. Since compulsory school attendance laws force teachers to do police work anyway, real teaching becomes more and more difficult. If you add to this the requirement to implement a regressive vision of education of the 'No More Fun in Schools' variety, teaching increasingly becomes a grim and repressive task. It would be in the teachers' best interests to do away with compulsion and establish instead what has been called elsewhere the 'invitational school'.

As regressive ideas came back into fashion, John Holt decided to work with the minority of more optimistic parents who wanted something different and who were active in setting up small alternative schools. These usually struggled because of the problems of finance. But some of these parents had begun to educate their children at home and needed support. Therefore, Holt established a service organization called Growing Without Schooling. Home-based education became the focus of his writing and activity.

The motives for home-based education

Holt gives three main reasons why people take their children out of school to educate them at home. (Others have listed as many as ten.) One is that the families decide that raising children is their business and not that of the government. A second is that the parents enjoy being with their children while watching them and helping them learn. They do not want to give this up to complete strangers called teachers. Third, they want to prevent their children from being unnecessarily hurt, whether mentally, spiritually or physically. All kinds of people can and do home-educate for one or more of the above reasons.

Some, like Holt himself, go on to question the notion of compulsory schooling as a serious infringement of civil liberties, even if the schools were to become more humane and effective. Holt developed a list of ten ways in which the civil liberties of children are violated, including secret record keeping and testing by compulsion:

There are a number of practices, by now very common in schools all over the country, which in and of themselves seriously violate the civil liberties of children, including:

1. Keeping permanent records of children's school performance. This would be inexcusable even if there were nothing in the records but academic grades. It is nobody's proper business that a certain child got a certain mark in a certain course when she or he was eight years old.
2. Keeping school records secret from children and/or their parents, a practice that continues in many places even where the law expressly forbids it.
3. Making these records available, without the permission of the children or their parents, to whoever may ask for them – employers, the police, the military, or other branches of government.
4. Filling these records, as experience has shown they are filled, with many kinds of malicious and derogatory information and misinformation. These may include not just unconfirmed teachers' reports of children's misbehavior, but also all kinds of pseudopsychological opinions, judgments, and diagnoses about the children and even their families. For examples, see *The Myth of the Hyper-active Child*, by Peter Schrag and Diane Divoky (New York: Pantheon Books, 1975).
5. Compulsory psychological testing of children, and including the results of these tests in children's records.
6. Labeling children as having such imaginary and supposedly incurable diseases as 'minimal brain dysfunction,' 'hyperactivity,' 'specific learning disabilities,' etc.
7. Compulsory dosing of children with very powerful and dangerous psychoactive drugs, such as Ritalin.
8. Using corporal punishment in school, which in practice often means the brutal beating of young children for very minor or imagined offenses.

9. Lowering students' academic grades, or even giving failing grades, solely for disciplinary and/or attendance reasons. Not only is this practice widespread, but school administrators openly boast of it, though what it amounts to in fact is the deliberate falsification of an official record, a kind of printed perjury.
10. In all of these matters, and indeed in almost any conflict between the child and the school, denying anything that could fairly be called 'due process'. (*Teach Your Own*, p. 20)

On the theme of protecting children from harm, the experience of families who see alert, lively-minded children become subdued and lose their sparkle and their smiles after starting school is a common reason for beginning to review the wisdom of agreeing to send them in the first place. Taking the children out of school is seen as preventing any further damage before a kind of healing takes place. Holt cites the case where it was the disappearance of a smile that led Ms O'Shea, a certified elementary school teacher, to question the value of public education:

When Kim was little, she was such a happy, laughy little person. When she went to school, that completely changed. She stopped smiling. She went for six months, and she was very unhappy. It was weird. When I went to the school, the teacher kept apologizing for the noise, and I thought, 'There's not any noise. These kids are like little robots.' (*Teach Your Own*, p. 33)

Common objections to home-based education

The case for home-based education was tackled by John Holt by dealing with the common questions he encountered in discussions and correspondence. The first of these is the 'social glue' question of whether the compulsory school is required to give a sense of unity to a fragmented population. Some kinds of community gathering and activity might help here, Holt says, but not the kind of schools we have now, which are set up to divide people into winners and losers, and prepare young people for a lifetime of winning or losing. The losers are then fated to look for others to look down on to make themselves feel a bit better. Home-based education is more hopeful: 'Most children who learn without school, or who go only when they want to, grow up with a much stronger sense of their own dignity and worth, and therefore, with much less need to despise and hate others' (*Teach Your Own*, p. 37). Such people can *afford* to be kind, patient, generous, forgiving and tolerant as a consequence of being people who are secure in having love and respect for themselves, and therefore have energy and concern that they can devote to others.

A second question is that of the 'social mixing' schools are said to provide. In reality, Holt observes, no such thing happens. Children spend most of their school hours in the same group of the same age, and since most schools eventually stream or set children for examination purposes, the experience of different people narrows as they get older. The result of this is commonly called 'the tyranny of the peer group', and the power of the youth culture that is formed in the process is a widely recognized phenomenon. It is not particularly surprising, therefore, that the research shows home-educated children are more emotionally secure, more independent, more socially skilled and more socially experienced. While the schooled are locked into each other's company for 15,000 hours or more, the home-educated are often out and about in society, mixing with all kinds of people.

A third and much more difficult question is that of parents with narrow visions. Holt starts from the proposition that in a free country, as opposed to a totalitarian or police state, as long as you obey the law you can believe what you like. The USA and its constitution were built on such tolerance. In any case, who is to say what is for certain true, and which set of ideas should be imposed? Schools act as if these issues have been decided, and yet many people are appalled at the outcome. Then there is the practical issue of whether schools are actually any good at changing attitudes:

> Even if we could agree that the school should try to stamp out narrow and bigoted ideas, we would still have to ask ourselves, does this work? Clearly it doesn't . . . If the schools were as good as they claim at stamping out prejudice, there ought not to be any left. A quick glance at any day's news will show that there is plenty left. (*Teach Your Own*, p. 42)

The next two questions are often asked close together but can be seen to cancel each other out. One is about school teaching children to fit into a mass society. The other is about school preventing children from being solely exposed to the values of a mass society by providing other values. School can either teach the values of the mass society or try to give an antidote. It cannot do both. In fact, Holt observes, schools are usually more concerned to induce conformity with mass society values than provide resistance to those values, as shown in the commonly expressed concern that children educated at home might become 'outsiders' or 'fail to adjust' to society.

The next question is often the first question people ask when startled by the news that some people prefer home-based education. It is 'If children are taught at home, won't they miss the valuable social life of the school?'

But it is social life that is often the *reason* why people pull their children out of school. Its quality is usually mean-spirited, competitive, exclusive, status-seeking, snobbish, and dominated by fad and fashion. Parents watch helplessly as their child becomes a stranger dominated by a variety of unhealthy peer-group influences: 'I remember my sister saying of one of her children, then five, that she never really did anything mean or silly until she went to school – a nice school, by the way, in a nice small town' (*Teach Your Own*, p. 45). In response to this analysis, Holt reports that not once did he encounter the response that he was completely mistaken and that the social life of school was kindly, generous, supportive, democratic, friendly, loving and good for children. The response was that this was what they would meet in Real Life, so they had better be toughened up and get used to it. 'Toughening up' often meant being persuaded to become a cigarette smoker or regular drinker, or to try drugs or petty crime:

> Of course, children who spend almost all of their time in groups of other people their own age, shut out of society's serious work and concerns, with almost no contact with adults except child-watchers, are going to feel that what 'all the other kids' are doing is the right, the best, the only thing to do. (*Teach Your Own*, p. 50).

In dealing with the question of children being taught by the unqualified, John Holt sets out to demystify teaching and learning. The fact is that there is no agreement among educators about what is good teaching, and the dismal record of schools is proof of this. Humans have been sharing information and skills with the young for centuries using a few simple commonsense ideas:

> For a long, long time, people who were good at sharing what they knew have realized certain things: (1) to help people learn something, you must first understand what they already know; (2) showing people how to do something is better than telling them and letting them do it is best of all; (3) you mustn't tell or show too much at once, since people digest new ideas slowly and must feel secure with new skills or knowledge before they are ready for more; (4) you must give people as much time as they want and need to absorb what you have shown or told them; (5) instead of testing their understanding with questions you must let them show how much or how little they understand by the questions they ask you; (6) you must not get impatient or angry when people do not understand; (7) scaring people only blocks learning, and so on. (*Teach Your Own*, p. 52)

Parents using these principles can cope as well as any certified teacher, and Holt quotes a court case in Kentucky where the verdict was that there was not 'a scintilla of evidence' that certificated teachers produced better results. The additional advantages to students learning at home are that their parents are not distracted by the problems of managing a class; they know the children better, including their spoken and unspoken signals, and they care more about them – they are not teaching in order to earn a salary. Also, they are not bound by the constipated knowledge formulas of school, for as one homeschooling mother wrote to John Holt after she had anxiously aped the school curriculum at home, her children protested that if they were going to have to spend their time 'doing this school junk', they would rather do it at school than poison the atmosphere at home.

But parents who offer their children the chance to have a home-based education need 'qualifications' other than teacher certification:

> We can sum up very quickly what people need to teach their own children. First of all, they have to like them, enjoy their company, their physical presence, their energy, foolishness, and passion. They have to enjoy all their talk and questions, and enjoy equally trying to answer those questions. They have to think of their children as friends, indeed very close friends, have to feel happier when they are near and miss them when they are away. They have to trust them as people, respect their fragile dignity, treat them with courtesy, take them seriously. They have to feel in their own hearts some of their children's wonder, curiosity, and excitement about the world. And they have to have enough confidence in themselves, skepticism about experts, and willingness to be different from most people, to take on themselves the responsibility for their children's learning. (*Teach Your Own*, p. 57)

Only a minority of parents start out with *all* these qualities. Some of them are gained or strengthened along the way. But most will have exercised many of these qualities in bringing up their young children, so they are not outside their capabilities or experience.

Other questions that crop up are dealt with by Holt. For example:

> 'How am I going to teach my child six hours a day?'

The answer given is that what they get at school is closer to 15 minutes a week of personal attention.

> 'I don't want to feel I am sheltering my children or running away from adversity.'

The answer given is that sheltering your children is your job as a parent. You would not starve your children just because many children in the world are starved, so if you think school is bad, you should give your children something better.

'I value their learning how to handle challenges and problems.'

Holt responds:

> To learn to know oneself, and to find a life worth living and work worth doing, is problem and challenge enough, without having to waste time on the fake and unworthy challenges of school – pleasing the teacher, staying out of trouble, fitting in with the gang, being popular, doing what everyone else does. (*Teach Your Own*, p. 64–5)

The politics of home-based education

Holt was concerned with some political aspects of home-based education. The first is the nature of social change. Important changes occur only when people change their lives, not their political parties or political beliefs. Thus, grassroots-inspired changes like more healthy eating inspired by vegetarians, or nonsmoking groups achieving smoking-free public places, or humanists pioneering nonreligious funerals, weddings and naming ceremonies for non-believers, occur in this way. People change their lives not because they lose an argument but because they come to decide in favor of action. It was for this reason that John Holt gave up arguing with educationalists in lectures and writing as a waste of time, and decided to seek out, and work with, those who wanted to change things. At first, this was the small-school movement, but small schools found it hard to survive and difficult to grow. Homeschoolers, however, could survive and grow. With help and support they did.

Holt proposes a different idea of leadership from the guru model. In grassroots social change everyone is a leader:

> Leaders are not what many people think – people with huge crowds following them. Leaders are people who go their own way without caring, or even looking to see whether anyone is following them. 'Leadership qualities' are not the qualities that enable people to attract followers, but those that enable them to do without them ... This is the opposite of the 'charisma' that we hear so much about. Charismatic leaders make us think, 'Oh, if only I could do that, be like that.' True leaders make us think, 'If they can do that ... I can do it too.' They do not make people into followers, but into new leaders. (*Teach Your Own*, p. 68)

Consequently, in the movement for home-based education, everyone becomes a general.

There are those who argue that parents should stay with schools and try to make them better. Those who plead thus often believe that schools were invented to give the poor a better chance. This is an illusion, Holt declares. Schools actually favor those already privileged. A few poor children do make it through the system, just enough to keep the myth alive and to fool people into thinking it is a fair race. Schools like to say they create and spread knowledge. It would be closer to the truth to say that they collect and hoard knowledge, corner the market on it if they can, so that they can sell it at the highest possible price. That is why they want everyone to believe that only what is learned at school is worth anything. But this idea, as much as any other, freezes the class structure of society and locks the poor into poverty.

Some working-class families believe they will be targeted by the authorities if they opt for home-based education. Holt responded that, in his experience, if the schools are in a hounding mood, they will hound anybody and, indeed, worry more about losing middle-class children who might do well in examinations. Nevertheless, bullies take on those they think are the weakest, so 'bullying' schools may see working-class families or single parents as an easy target, and this does sometimes happen. Holt's Growing Without Schooling group tried to give the necessary support when this happened.

How to opt out of schooling

Holt provided practical advice for parents on how to get started. There are ideas for preparing their letters and documents to present their case for homeschooling to schools and education authorities. There are model letters and some of the official replies that resulted. I know from my experience in the UK that the advice given is sound and works. The process of preparing the case and getting it down in writing is itself a confidence-building experience. Many families report that *making the decision* turns out to be the most difficult thing. Preparing the case and then getting their program operational turns out to be much more straightforward than they could ever have believed.

Further practical advice from homeschoolers is given as to how to set about their programs, whether structured (which means preplanned), unstructured (which really means emergent structures based on exploration, since no learning is unstructured) or a mixture of the two approaches. This leads into some ideas about the principles of living with children in the regular and intense way that homeschooling requires.

Anticipating the work of Alice Miller in books like *For Your Own Good*: *Hidden Cruelty in Child-Rearing and the Roots of Violence* (translated by Hildegarde and Hunter Hannum, London: Virago, 1987), Holt proposed that one of the most deep-rooted of the causes of our present problems is the way we treat children. The reactionary and the romantic views of children are both firmly rejected. One approach says we should 'force the badness out of them' or exercise some other version of 'tough love'; the other says we should not influence them because this 'squeezes the natural goodness out of them'. Holt advocated an approach based on reasoning, feeling it to be better than either of these ideas. I have to say, he is entirely vindicated in his approach in my own experience of teaching and parenting. The experience of home-based education in the UK is that the most confident, courteous and independent-minded children have been subject to this kind of approach.

Lifeschool

Home-based educators have the opportunity to pursue real learning in the real world, or 'lifeschool'. This is an advantage over almost all schools, for even in 'free' or alternative schools there is too much tendency to defer to what conventional schools do by taking learners away from the great richness and variety of the real world and replacing it with an artificial and contrived learning environment. As one parent puts it, '"Susan lives in a world of marvelous *abundance*; her resources are unlimited. She has not been 'socialized' by school to think that education is a supply of scarce knowledge to be competed for by hungry, controlled children"' (*Teach Your Own*, p. 169). Another family stressed the incidental learning of everyday events. They planned a special 'educational' field trip once a week as part of their learning programe. These were fun and not without value, but the phoniness and rigidity of their ritual finally got to the family and they stopped doing it as a routine. The weekly trips to the town to shop, use the library, the bank, the post office and other local facilities became more valued as a result.

This led Holt to suggest that the country club remodeled as a family club would be a better expenditure of public money than schools. There would be no curriculum, just facilities and opportunities for meeting, living and doing things. Only a few schools operate like this, and one appears to be Sudbury Valley School in Framingham, Massachusetts. As one parent observed, any young person who has been to the usual type of school knows that school is only a euphemism for a children's day prison.

Holt emphasizes the idea that play is serious for learners; in particular, it is young children's *work*. Included are several accounts from families relating to this theme. This leads into one of John Holt's main themes, that of learning without teaching. Learning is defined in a quite straightforward way as 'finding out'. He suggests that it may wound us a little to realize that children can often get along very well as learners without adult help and that if they need it, they will ask for it.

He refers back to his proposition in *How Children Fail* that it was fear, boredom and the confusion of having constantly to manipulate meaningless words and symbols that made children stupid, and adds a further insight:

> I now see that it was that, but far more than that, the fact that *others had taken control of their minds*. It was being *taught*, in the sense of being trained like circus animals to do tricks on demand, that had made them stupid (at least in school)... The most important question any thinking creature can ask itself is, 'What is worth thinking about?' When we deny its right to decide for itself, when we try to control what it must attend to and think about, we make it less observant, resourceful, and adaptive, in a word, less intelligent, in a blunter word, more stupid. (*Teach Your Own*, p. 231)

Learning difficulties

Dyslexia and problems with left and right identification are two of the learning difficulties explored by Holt. His experience as a teacher and his reflections on that experience led him to argue that learning difficulties are usually created, or at least amplified, by the school:

> Parents should be extremely skeptical of anything the school and their specialists may say about their children and their condition and needs. Above all, they should understand that it is almost certainly the school itself and all its tensions and anxieties that are causing these difficulties, and that the best treatment for them will probably be to take the child out of school altogether. (*Teach Your Own*, p. 233)

Children and work

A job is something you do for money. A career is a ladder of jobs. Work is something worth doing for its own sake, something you might do for money or do even if the work did not pay. Few young people give a hopeful, positive or enthusiastic response to the last one. They can only envisage a job. This limited vision that their society has given them increasingly dominates learning as students grow older, for John Holt finds that the key question they ask is 'What do you have to do to pass the course?' This is closely linked to the assumption that a job may result from the course. Enjoyment and satisfaction frequently have nothing to do with it:

> A young woman about to graduate from a school of education once said to me, 'Well, I've learned two things here, anyway – that I don't like children and I don't like teaching.' I asked why she went on with it. She said, 'I have to, I've spent too much time and money learning to do this, I can't turn around and start to learn to do something else'. (*Teach Your Own*, p. 254)

Home-based education gives a chance to break with this negative view of jobs and work and the related attitude to learning, and do something more optimistic.

The findings of the courts and legal strategies

Home-based education has been the subject of many court actions in the USA. Although the detailed findings are specific to US law, the general findings are of more widespread interest:

1. Parents have a right to educate their children in whatever way they believe in; the state cannot impose on all parents any kind of educational monopoly, of schools, methods or aims.
2. The state may not deprive parents of this right for arbitrary reasons, but only for serious educational ones, which it must make known to parents, with all the forms of due process.
3. A state that would deny parents these rights by saying that their home education plan is inadequate has a burden of proof to show beyond reasonable doubt that this is so. Parents are assumed to be competent to teach their children until proved otherwise.
4. In order to show that the parents' educational plans are inadequate, the state must show that its own requirements and regulations are education-ally necessary and do in fact produce, in its own schools, better results than the parents get or are likely to get.

Holt gives a list of questions about what schools are doing and achieving that would make this last point very difficult to prove.

Holt advises parents to resist an attempt to have their children measured by standardized tests. Making small concessions about the curriculum may be tolerated for the sake of harmony, but no concessions should be made over tests, for these reasons:

(1) Even in the narrow area which they cover, the tests do not measure well what they claim to measure; (2) the tests do not touch those many areas outside the narrow school curriculum in which children may be learning a great deal. (*Teach Your Own*, p. 302)

Advice to schools

The final part of the book is directed to schools and how they should respond to the growing homeschooling movement. The first recommendation is not to panic, for even with full school cooperation and support, Holt estimates that the number of homeschooled is not likely to exceed ten per cent of the schooled population. Most school-age children are likely to continue in schools, hopefully reformed to become more educational and less custodial. There are simply not enough parents who either like or trust their children enough for it to be otherwise. It is not just attendance laws that keep children in schools. The adult population in general wants it that way; people want children to be out of the way during the daytime.

The main reason schools should cooperate with homeschooling is to learn from the experience of the families and how they get such good results:

> Homeschoolers will not teach the schools what they so yearn to know, the *one best way* to do anything. What they will teach is that there is no one best way, and that it is a waste of time and energy to look for it; that children (like adults) learn in a great many different ways; that each child learns best in the ways that most interest, excite, and satisfy her or him; and that the business of the school should be to offer the widest possible range of choices, both in what to learn and ways to learn it. (*Teach Your Own*, p. 331)

Schools lack good feedback, and homes can provide some. Homeschooled children who come to school on a flexitime basis will bring with them many ideas, skills, activities and resources to share with other children. In doing this, Holt predicts, they will make the school a different, nicer and more interesting place. Few people at present see schools as places they would go to by choice.

> Very few people now feel that way. Even when most people still supported the schools in principle, hundreds of parents, many of whom had even been good students, were telling or writing me that most of their worst anxiety dreams were still school dreams, or that every time they went into [their] children's school, for whatever reason, they could feel their insides tighten up and their hands begin to sweat. Many kinds of

places – concert halls, baseball parks, theaters, parks, beaches, to name but a few – make most people feel good as soon as they step into them. They think that something pleasant, interesting, exciting is about to happen. For their very survival, schools *need* people who feel that way about them. (*Teach Your Own*, p. 338)

In making these comments, Holt echoes the distinction made by Illich when he distinguishes between coercive institutions based on compulsion, and convivial ones based on choice. As regards teacher education, Holt proposes that a spell working with a homeschooling family would be very stimulating for students and teachers who choose it. This has been tried out in the UK at Birmingham University, where it proved to be of benefit to both parties.

For his final comments, John Holt emphasizes that homeschooling is a misnomer, for what it refers to is not a school at all but a place of natural learning, a place of home-based education. Schools need to move in this direction: 'What I am trying to say, in short, is that our chief educational problem is not to find a way to make homes more like schools. If anything, it is to make schools less like schools' (*Teach Your Own*, p. 347).

Chapter 12

Learning All the Time

Early in 1982, John Holt began work on what was to be his final book, *Learning All the Time*. Developing the interest in, and support for, parents opting to educate their children at home that he had demonstrated in *Teach Your Own*, the book was to be about how children learn to read and write and count at home, with very little or no teaching. By the spring of 1983 he had established clearly the purpose of the new book:

> The book will be a demonstration that children, without being coerced or manipulated, or being put in exotic, specially prepared environments, or having their thinking planned and ordered for them, can, will, and do pick up from the world around them important information about what we call the Basics.
>
> It will also demonstrate that 'ordinary' people, without special training and often without large amounts of schooling themselves, can give their children whatever slight assistance may be needed to help them in their exploration of the world, and that to do this task requires no more than a little tact, patience, attention, and readily available information. (*Learning All the Time*, p. xv)

He died in September 1985 with the book drafted but not finally edited. His colleagues at Holt Associates took on the task of editing and publishing the book, guided by the instructions they had received from John. Because he had given such clear instructions and had written the bulk of it already, it was possible to assemble the book and be confident that it was close to what John had intended. The few gaps were filled by editing in other articles and pieces he had written, but the main activity was to be editing down the wealth of material. John had anticipated this, proposing that 'cutting and squeezing, not puffing up', was going to be the task. The publishers acknowledged the skill of Holt Associates and others in preparing the manuscript:

The publishers wish to thank Nancy Wallace and Susannah Sheffer for much thoughtful editorial assistance. We are also grateful to Pat Farenga, Donna Richoux, and all the staff of Holt Associates for considerable help in making this publication possible. Each of these close colleagues and friends of John Holt's is involved in furthering his ideas and beliefs and helped us shoulder the difficult responsibility of editing and publishing a posthumous book. (*Learning All the Time*, p. xvii)

In order that his purpose would not be misinterpreted, John wrote a long letter in June 1984, which contained this key passage:

This is not a book about 'How to Help Your Child Succeed in School'. It is a book about children learning. By learning I mean making more sense of the world around them. (Let me try this again.) Learning, to me, means making more sense of the world around us, and being able to do more things in it. Success in school means remembering the answers to teachers' questions, getting clever about guessing what questions they will ask, and how to fool them when you don't know the answers.

Early in his teaching career, Holt was for a time tutoring an eighth-grader who was having some troubles in school. One day she asked him, with great seriousness, about how to learn history. Taking her question as seriously as she meant it, he said that she was probably asking two questions: one, how do I learn more about history, and two, how do I get better grades in history class in school? The first thing was to understand that these are completely different and separate activities, having almost nothing to do with each other. If you want to learn how to find out about what things were like in the past, there are ways of doing this. And if you want to find out how to get better grades in your history class, there are ways of doing that too. But they are not the same task. She understood and accepted this, and asked Holt for both kinds of suggestions, which he gave her.

In this final book, Holt for the most part discussed the first of these two questions: what sorts of things might we do to make various aspects of the world more accessible, interesting and transparent to children. The themes addressed are those of reading and writing, numbers and arithmetic, music, advice for parents, the learning style of young children, and a summary of the nature of learning. John Holt's style of writing makes the material very accessible, and parents, young teachers and seasoned educationalists all find the messages clear and intelligible. Because he stays close to experience most of the time, rarely deriving theory from theory, his ideas have immediate appeal.

Reading and writing

The chapter on reading and writing uses the familiar Holt technique of assembling observations and cases of children actually learning to read. From these he draws out his principles of learning to read. He notes how children learn best when they are comfortable and that sometimes this means close physical contact. As touching children becomes more frowned upon in schools, homes win out in providing this feature. But it is not only the probable absence of 'cozy physical contact' in classrooms that can inhibit learning to read, it is the public scrutiny of a child's performance that can have negative effects:

> Whether you are a 'gifted' five-year-old or a terrified, illiterate twelve-year-old, trying to read something new is a dangerous adventure. You may make mistakes, or fail, and so feel disappointment or shame, or anger, or disgust. Just in order to get started on this adventure, most people need as much comfort, reassurance, and security as they can find. The typical classroom with other children ready to point out, correct, and even laugh at every mistake, and the teacher all too often (willingly or unwillingly) helping and urging them to do this, is the worst possible place to begin. (*Learning All the Time*, p. 3)

The figure of 30 hours needed to learn to read is offered – provided the conditions are positive and not inhibiting. This figure was quoted by a Danish teacher, had cropped up again in adult literacy classes and had been put forward by the Brazilian Paulo Freire in his experience of teaching reading to illiterate peasant adults. Thirty hours is one school week, and this is the true size of the task, Holt proposes. It is not a difficult task unless we make it so: 'Learning to read is easy, and most children will do it more quickly and better and with more pleasure if they can do it themselves, untaught, untested, and helped only when and if they ask for help' (*Learning All the Time*, p. 8). Holt conceded that this view was not popular with the experts who make a living out of the teaching of reading; they have 'advocated a great many foolish things'. The idea of 'reading readiness' is singled out for comment. Showing children lots of books made up of pictures and asking silly questions about them is a mistake. What children need to get ready for reading, Holt argues, is exposure to a lot of print – not pictures, but print. The process is akin to that of learning to talk when children were surrounded by talk; they began to identify patterns in the jumble of sounds around them and take possession of some of the words:

They need to bathe their eyes in print, as when smaller they bathe their ears in talk. After a while, as they look at more and more print, these meaningless forms, curves, and squiggles begin to steady down, take shape, become recognisable, so that the children, without yet knowing what letters and words are, begin to see, as I once did myself, after looking at a page of print in an Indian typeface, that this letter appears here, and that group of letters appears there, and again here. When they've learned to see the letters and words, they are ready to ask themselves questions about what they mean and what they say. (*Learning All the Time*, p. 12)

This exposure to lots of print can take many forms. The large-print edition of the *New York Times* is recommended for US parents and teachers. Other print material from the adult world can be assembled: official forms, timetables, newspapers, magazines, instruction manuals, leaflets, handbills, telephone directories (especially yellow pages directories), road maps, letters and posters. Dictionaries, on the other hand, are overrated, since most people acquire big vocabularies by working out the meanings from the context and not by consulting dictionaries. In his lifetime, Holt reckoned, he had consulted dictionaries only about 50 times in total:

The trouble with telling children what words mean, or asking them to ask the dictionary to tell them, is that they don't get a chance to figure out the meaning of the word. Figuring out what you don't know or aren't sure of is the greatest intellectual skill of all. (*Learning All the Time*, p. 20)

Next, we are moved on to look at the issue of phonics. Holt is in favor of 'sensible phonics' but identifies most of the phonics cult as nonsense that just gets in the way of successful reading. One reading expert identified 500 reading skills, later reduced to 273. Holt proposes that there are only two general ideas that need to be grasped, and they are, first, that written letters stand for spoken sounds, and second, that the order of the letters on the page, from our left to our right, corresponds to the order in time of the spoken sounds. Children do not need to recite these rules, only to know how to apply them. In addition:

Aside from that, what children have to learn are the connections between the 45 or so sounds that make up spoken English and the 380 or so letters or combinations of letters that represent these sounds in written English. This is not a large or a hard task. But, as in everything else, the schools do a great deal to make it larger and harder. (*Learning All the Time*, p. 23)

The first mistake is to teach the sounds of each individual letter. This is false information, especially in the case of consonants, where only six or seven can be said by themselves, with four borderline cases, and the rest have a sound only if combined with a vowel in a word or syllable. Vowels have variable sounds depending on which consonants or combination of consonants they are associated with, so teaching these as sounds in isolation is also foolish. In addition, the actual definition of what counts as a vowel and a consonant is inconsistent.

The reading books used in schools are identified as a major obstacle to learning to read. Holt felt that the books that most children are compelled to learn to read from are boring, stupid, shallow, misleading, dishonest and unreal (*Learning All the Time*, p. 28).

In his tribute to Holt, George Dennison said that John was never unkind to his opponents. This has always worried me, personally, since it puts intolerable burdens on the rest of us trying to continue the tradition of constructive doubt, and the questioning of the dogmas of schooling in particular and education in general. It is hard to feel kindly disposed to people who do so much damage by flouting both reason and evidence. So, it is with some relief that I find that Holt does not disguise his scorn in this instance at least.

Some interesting statistics are introduced to make the point about reading books. In 1920, the readers available contained an average of 645 words. This number was reduced to 460 in the 1930s, to 350 in the 1940s and to between 113 and 173 in the 1960s. The explanation Holt offers is that as the readers became more and more boring, children learned to read less and less well. Children had a harder time working up an interest in this stuff and therefore in learning to read. The experts, however, concluded that the books were too difficult for children rather than too boring to hold their interest, and so set to make them easier – and made them more boring than ever.

The other mistake that schools make is identified by Holt as making children read aloud in class. This inhibits the natural process of self-correction of mistakes. Self-correction occurs in private reading with a sympathetic adult or other child, and in silent reading. But reading out loud in class puts a premium on getting it right first time or suffering the consequences of public exposure, amusement or worse. In this matter, Holt returned to the theme of his first book on how children learn to fail in the relatively learning-hostile arena of the classroom.

In learning to read, another obstacle put in the way of children is the pretense that the language conventions are self-evident and reasonable when in fact they are often arbitrary and inconsistent. Holt wrote that there is nothing self-evident or natural or reasonable about it at all. We just do it that way. But nothing makes school more mysterious, meaningless, baffling and terrifying to a child than constantly hearing adults tell him or her things as if they were simple, self-evident, natural and logical, when in fact they are quite the reverse: arbitrary, contradictory, obscure and often absurd, flying in the face of a child's common sense (*Learning All the Time*, p. 32).

In a short section on spelling, there are a number of practical suggestions about how accurate spelling might be encouraged, but they are all linked to the proposition that the best way to spell better is to read a lot and write a lot:

> People who spell badly – I have taught many of them – are not much helped by rules and drills. In all my work as a teacher, nothing I ever did to help bad spellers was as effective as not doing anything, except telling them to stop worrying about it, and to get on with their reading and writing. (*Learning All the Time*, p. 36)

As regards handwriting, Holt questioned the whole notion of cursive handwriting, seeing it as something of a superstition. He found to his surprise that the students in his classes who wrote most quickly and legibly used manuscript printing. He proved to himself in some experiments in his classes that print was more legible and also faster. So where did the idea of joining up writing come from? It appears to persist purely out of a bad habit. John Holt decided to drop cursive writing from his own set of habits and taught himself manuscript printing instead. As far as he could tell, cursive writing evolved from an elaborate script invented for the slow process of engraving in copper. Some people, somewhere, decided to impose this style on children, and so we are stuck with a bad idea. In the real world of typing, word processing and printing, of course, such a silly idea is ignored. (Nobody is yet daft enough to impose joined-up figures in arithmetic on children, but give it time . . .)

'At Home with Numbers'

The section 'At Home with Numbers' begins with the mischievous suggestion that if arithmetic were illegal, children would probably learn it, and learn it better. Since so many adults have trouble with numbers, something must go wrong quite early on. Holt suggests that abstraction is introduced too soon and too often. Although numbers are abstract, they are abstractions of something and without that something, meaninglessness can soon follow:

> For this reason, it seems to me extremely important that children not be taught to count number names in the absence of real objects . . . or put it differently, when little children first meet numbers they should always

meet them as adjectives not nouns. It should not at first be 'three', or 'seven', all by itself, but always 'two coins', or 'three matches', or 'four spoons', or whatever it may be. (*Learning All the Time*, p. 47)

Children can be confused by isolated number facts, he continues, and four different ways of looking at the same fact should not be taught as if they were four unrelated facts. Thus, $2 + 3 = 5, 3 + 2 = 5, 5 - 2 = 3$ and $5 - 3 = 2$ are one number fact looked at in four different ways. The one fact can be expressed as ***** = *** **.

Once children have discovered this set of relationships, they can discover the same things about any number. Since discovering for ourselves is more powerful than being told and then memorizing, and in any case is more fun, learning is more efficient.

The section continues with John Holt giving a range of practical ways of helping children become confident with numbers. There is the 'home-made adding machine' and various grid games for learning tables. There are ideas on learning to multiply large numbers and how to cope with fractions. He talks about 'bootleg maths' – the world of puzzles children try on each other furtively – and thus returns to his joke that if maths were illegal, children would learn it better.

In 'family economics', he suggests that children should know, or be able to know, about the finances of their families. This is introducing numbers and arithmetic in a real context which leads on to ideas such as interest, loans, percentages, installments, mortgages and insurance.

In a section on solving problems, Holt's approach to learning mathematics becomes clear. Mathematics should be seen as fascinating and beautiful; it also has a few practical uses in solving some everyday problems. Above all, he argues, it should be *fun*. In meetings of teachers he always met those who angrily disagreed with this idea:

It often happens that someone says, usually in an angry tone of voice, 'Learning can't be all fun!' (what they usually mean by this is 'Learning can't ever be fun, or it isn't really learning'). They are so wrong about this. Figuring things out, solving problems, is about as much fun as anything we human beings know how to do. For pleasure and excitement, hardly anything beats it, and few things come close. (*Learning All the Time*, p. 83)

Young children as research scientists

Holt moves on to the central theme of his work about how children learn. He sees them as born learners who turn experience into knowledge by the same methods as research scientists. They observe their surroundings, they speculate and wonder, and they ask themselves questions. They formulate possible answers, make theories, hypothesize and test out their ideas in various ways. Insensitive adults can and do eradicate this natural learning, especially in the kind of schools we have established: 'If we attempt to control, manipulate, or divert this process, we disturb it. If we continue this long enough, the process stops. The independent scientist in the child disappears' (*Learning All the Time*, p. 95).

Loving music

As a musician himself, and one who learned the cello late in his life, in his fifties, John Holt had decided views about learning music. His experience led him to question many of the dogmas about musical education. The first one he questions is this: if you do not start early, it is too late. Not only did this contradict his own personal experience in becoming a competent cello player in his fifties, but he recalls how a manager of a professional-class civic orchestra confirmed that many of the musicians she worked with were late starters who did not begin until well into their twenties and later. The myth of 'if you do not start early, you might as well not start at all' operates as a self-fulfilling prophecy because the music institutions often base their activity on that assumption.

A second notion that Holt questioned is that of the 'need to practice'. Why talk about practice at all? Why not just talk about playing the instrument? For professional musicians the matter is clear, for playing for an audience is 'playing' and preparing to play for an audience is 'practice', but for amateurs the distinction is not valid. Amateurs just play their instruments, either by themselves or with others. If they do not enjoy it, the point of doing it is lost:

> We need to take serious account of the fact, well known to most musicians, that most children who have been to any great degree pushed into music, however skilful they may become at it, do not enjoy it very much. A number of my professional musician friends have said wistfully that they wished they loved music as much as I do. (*Learning All the Time*, p. 113)

The work of Suzuki in Japan appealed to Holt, and he was also concerned about some of the distortions of Suzuki's ideas. The method made sense to Holt because it relies on the same approach as the one children used to learn their native language. Parents were to play recordings at home as often as possible, recordings of expert violinists playing the simple violin tunes so that children would get to know them. When the child was 3, one of the parents would start violin lessons, taking the child with them. If in due course the child showed interest in playing too, a child-sized violin would be produced so that they could join in. Later, they could have the opportunity to join other children who had learned the same tunes, and in due course be introduced to musical notation, having learned to play by ear until then:

> When a group of these children came to the New England Conservatory on a tour of the US, I was there to hear them, along with several hundred others, many of them music teachers. The children, perhaps twenty of them, came on-stage, healthy, energetic, and happy. At the time I thought the average age of the children might be five or six; I now think they may have been a year or two older. Dr. Suzuki and a young assistant checked the tuning of the children's violins. We waited in great suspense. What would they play? Perhaps some of the slower and easier tunes of Vivaldi, Handel, or Bach? Dr. Suzuki gave the downbeat, and then away they went – playing not some easy tune but the Bach Double Concerto, in perfect time, tempo and rhythm, and with great energy and musicality. It was breathtaking, hair-raising. I could not have been more astonished if the children had floated up to the ceiling. Rarely in my life have I seen or heard anything so far beyond the bounds of what I would have thought possible. (*Learning All the Time*, pp. 115–16)

Sadly, Holt observed, the Suzuki method had become rigid in the hands of traditional music teachers who failed to understand the logistics of the approach. The exploration, discovery, adventure, joy and excitement of the original Suzuki approach had once again been slowly strangled and then replaced by formal and rigid instruction. This compulsion and rigidity has a price, he argued, for it does for Beethoven and Mozart what many schools already do to Shakespeare.

What parents can do

John Holt tells us how, when he was 4 years old, he and his sister used to slip out of bed and settle down at the top of the stairs to listen to the adult conversations going on below. He notes that young children learn so much from adult conversation. The one clear advantage the adults have is that they have been around longer and therefore have more experience and have some mental maps of the world around them. The *way* that they make that experience available is crucial:

What adults can do for children is to make more and more of that world and the people in it accessible and transparent to them. The key word is access: to people, places, experiences, the places where we work, other places we go – cities, countries, streets, buildings. We can also make available tools, books, records, toys, and other resources. (*Learning All the Time*, p. 127)

Parents can help by answering questions honestly but avoiding the trap of using every question as an excuse to do some teaching. Answer the question and leave it at that, for if more information is needed, it will be requested. The child who was assigned to read a book on penguins in school wrote in his report that the book said more about penguins than he wanted to know. We must be aware of the dangers of penguinizing, says Holt. He gives a further illustration of the child who exhausted her mother's knowledge and was advised to ask her father. The child replied, 'Well, I don't want to know that much about it.' A radical lesson is drawn from all this:

Not only is it the case that uninvited teaching does not make learning, but – and this was even harder for me to learn – for the most part such teaching prevents learning. Now that's a real shocker. Ninety-nine percent of the time, teaching that has not been asked for will not result in learning, but will impede learning. (*Learning All the Time*, p. 128)

The reason is that uninvited teaching carries hidden messages. One is that you are not smart enough to see that this is important. Another is that you will probably not bother to find out unless I teach it to you. A third is that I need to teach you because it is difficult and you are not smart enough to sort it out for yourself. These are messages of distrust and even contempt. The problem is that we like teaching, and that we are teaching animals as well as learning animals (*Learning All the Time*, p. 129).

But we have to restrain that impulse and the need to explain things to everybody ... until we are asked. Even then we have to answer sparingly and sensitively. People who do not see this are often the same people who want 'more structure' to get children learning. This usually means some adult telling children what to do and how to do it. Only the structure of the task is legitimate, Holt proposed, not the will of the adult. To get the sense of the process by which good work is done, they need to watch adults or others and to learn by the power of example. Cooking, typing, drawing, gardening, woodworking, car maintenance are all everyday examples of the opportunity to learn about structure. Workplaces are particular places that Holt wanted to see opened up to children to gain these kinds of experiences.

Next, John Holt seemed to begin to do the task I set myself in writing this book, for he begins to draw in ideas from several of his books to advise readers on how to help their children learn. The close and sympathetic observation of children is stressed and the need to go with the flow of children's learning. Interfering with their styles of learning is likely to be counterproductive and lead to the self-defeating behaviors he described in *How Children Fail*. In *How Children Learn* and again in *Teach Your Own*, he had warned about the over-anxious correction of mistakes, which destroys the slower but more effective self-correcting processes. We fool ourselves if we think corrections are not received as reproofs and therefore lead to the weakening of confidence:

> It is always, without exception, better for a child to figure out something on his own than to be told – provided, of course, as in the matter of running across the street, that his life is not endangered in the learning. But in matters intellectual, I admit no exception to this rule. In the first place, what he figures out, he remembers better. In the second place, and far more important, every time he figures something out, he gains in confidence in his ability to figure things out. (*Learning All the Time*, p. 138)

Next, Holt asked the question 'How much praise do children need?' A little goes a long way, is his answer, because too much praise creates 'praise junkies'. Children who get too much praise become dependent on continued adult approval and eventually frightened to make mistakes. The trouble with any external motivation is that it displaces or submerges internal motivation. If we praise them for everything they do that pleases us, they will learn to do things just to please us rather than for their own satisfaction, and then get worried about not pleasing us:

> What children want and need from us is thoughtful attention. They want us to notice them and pay some kind of attention to what they do, to take them seriously, to trust and respect them as human beings. They want courtesy and politeness, but they don't need much praise. (*Learning All the Time*, pp. 140–1)

But adults need not hold back from making suggestions, provided it is clear that they are suggestions and that the child is free to reject them. Adults must learn to take 'no' for an answer to some, and maybe quite a lot, of their endless stream of helpful suggestions.

The nature of learning

In his final chapter, John Holt started with three misleading metaphors about education. The first is the idea that education is an assembly line in a bottling plant. Pupils are seen as empty containers coming down the conveyor belt. The teachers are stationed along the assembly line at intervals and squirt various amounts of different subjects over the containers as they pass on during their 15,000-hour journey down the conveyor belt. The management decides what substances and in what quantities are to be squirted, how much at a time, and what is to be done about those containers that do fill up sufficiently.

The question of why so many of the containers leave the long journey down the conveyor belt more or less empty, or leak out their contents soon after leaving the factory, is not seriously addressed, because of the persistent belief that squirting actually works – that is, that teaching, seen as squirting adult-imposed knowledge at pupils, actually produces learning: 'If students don't know enough, we insist, it is because we didn't start squirting soon enough (start them at four) or didn't squirt the right stuff, or enough of it (toughen up the curriculum)' (*Learning All the Time*, p. 149).

The second metaphor sees students as laboratory rats in a cage, being trained to do some kind of trick, usually of a kind they would not perform in real life. If the rat presses the right levers, it is rewarded by a morsel of food; if not, it is punished by being given an electric shock. The sequence is task–morsel or shock, or task–carrot or stick, or task–positive reinforcement or negative reinforcement:

> The positive reinforcements in schools are teachers' smiles, gold stars, 'A's on report cards, dean's lists, and entrance into prestigious colleges, good jobs, interesting work, money and success. The negative reinforcements are angry scoldings, sarcasm, contempt, humiliation, shame, the derisive laughter of other children, the threats of failure, of being held back, of flunking out of school ... at the end of this line are entrance to low-rank colleges or none at all, bad jobs or none at all, dull work if any, not much money or outright poverty. (*Learning All the Time*, p. 150)

The third metaphor is that of school as a mental hospital, a treatment institution. If the children do not learn what is presented, they are lazy, disorganized or mentally disturbed. They may have 'learning disabilities', or 'perceptual handicaps', or 'school phobia', or something. This kind of explanation is popular because it gets everybody off the hook. Anxious middle-class parents can be reassured that they did nothing wrong; it is just that their child has some wires crossed in his or her head. Demands for schools to do better can be set aside with explanations about the numbers of the 'learning disabled' in the school:

> The 'research' behind these labels is biased and not very persuasive. Some years ago, at a large conference of specialists in learning disability, I asked whether anyone had heard of – not done, but merely heard of – any research linking so-called perceptual handicaps with stress. In the audience of about 1,100, two hands were raised. One man told me then, the other told me later, about research that showed that when students with supposedly severe learning disabilities were put in a relatively stress-free situation, *their disabilities soon vanished.* (*Learning All the Time*, p. 151)

All these metaphors distract us from the truth that children are natural learners who get better and better at learning unless adults start preventing them from doing so. Such adults may have good intentions but bad understanding. They do not understand about natural learning. Learning, like breathing, is not an act of volition for children. They do not think, 'Now I shall set to and learn this'. It is their nature to look about them, to take the world in with their senses and to make sense out of it, without knowing that they are doing it or how they are doing it. Holt concluded that the idea that we can teach young children how to learn is utterly absurd:

> Children are not only extremely good at learning; they are much better at it than we are. As a teacher, it took me a long time to find this out. I was an ingenious and resourceful teacher, clever about thinking up lesson plans and demonstrations and motivating devices and all of that acamaracus. And I only very slowly and painfully – believe me, painfully – learned that when I started teaching less, the children started learning more. I can sum up in five to seven words what I eventually learned as a teacher. The seven word version is: Learning is not the product of teaching. The five word version is: Teaching does not make learning . . . organised education operates on the assumption that children learn only when and only what and only because we teach them. This is not true. It is very close to one hundred percent false. (*Learning All the Time*, p. 160)

Adults may think they are introducing efficiency into children's natural methods of learning, but usually they slow their learning down and then eliminate the natural methods altogether. They then replace them with something that clearly does not work:

> What is efficient? How does a small child learn language? She absorbs with her ears an enormous amount of verbal information – if she is living in a family where she hears a lot of talk and where people talk to her. Most

of it she doesn't remember or doesn't even understand. But she picks out a bit here, a bit there. She picks out the things she wants and needs. We say, 'Ha, this is inefficient. When we get her in school, we're going to show her the efficient way to study language.' We have grammar, our tenses, vocabulary lists. But which is more efficient? Who learn languages better? (*Learning All the Time*, p. 154)

John Holt wanted to rescue learning from the myth-makers. He proposed that 'In short, what we need to know to help children learn is not obscure, technical, or complicated, and the materials we can use to help them lie ready at hand all around us' (*Learning All the Time*, p. 162).

Chapter 13

Growing Without Schooling

In 1977, the magazine *Growing Without Schooling* (GWS) was published for the first time. It was the first US magazine devoted to home-based education. The first edition was in the form of a four-page newsletter. The typeface was small, to allow four columns per page, and there were no illustrations. Later it grew to 12 pages, and later still it was revised to include illustrations.

The magazine was, in effect, John Holt's declaration that he had given up having anything to do with schools. In his book *Teach Your Own*, he had made his view clear that the best learning environment for a child was not in a school, however humane, but in a supportive home. He wrote that school was not a good idea gone wrong but a wrong idea from the word go.

Growing Without Schooling was published by Holt Associates out of Holt's crowded office in Boston, and its intentions were clear from the start. It would be a newsletter about ways in which people of any age can learn and do things, acquire skills, and find interesting and useful work without having to go through schooling. It would come out as often as there were interesting things to report, possibly only three or four times a year at first.

Schools would not feature much as a concern – not even small schools or alternative schools – but attention would be given to the concerns of those home-based educating families who decided that they needed 'school tickets' such as credits, certificates, degrees or diplomas.

From time to time, the GWS writers might have to argue with the school-bound majority to try to stop them from doing immediate harm, but mostly such arguing was seen as a waste of time. One running argument that could not be avoided, however, was on the theme of socialization.

On this theme, Holt and GWS took no prisoners. The social life of schools was rarely anything but mean-spirited, competitive, exclusive, status-seeking, an agenda set by the schools and copied by the peer group. A letter was quoted from a parent who had watched their youngster deteriorate from being a person into someone under peer influence. And Holt's own sister had said of one of her children that she did nothing really mean until she went to school and learned how to do it from her 'nice' school in a 'nice' small town. Socialization, given the nature of the social life in school, was reason enough to home-educate, though there were plenty of other reasons too.

There was advice on offer on issues such as 'what to say to the neighbors'. Holt suggested that parents might try saying that their child was on a special program that was rather new and that 'they' did not really want me to talk about it at this stage – all of which was close to the truth. Home-based education has grown so much in size and in public awareness since 1977, however, that it is doubtful whether this line would work anymore.

Parents who worried about teaching for six hours a day to match school hours were given a blunt reply. Who is teaching them for six hours a day anywhere? If they get 15 minutes' genuine teaching a day, it is unusual. Holt was referring to 'concerned and thoughtful adult talk' about something that the learner found interesting or important, rather than uninvited teaching of the 'stand and deliver' type.

The first GWS ended with a report about parents who had sued local schools because, after their children had spent years in them, they had learned nothing. A judge on the West Coast of the USA had thrown out the case on the grounds that the schools had no legal obligation to teach anyone anything. (The parents in the case, as I recall, were far from dismayed at this verdict but saw it as a victory.)

The second edition of GWS took a radical stance on leadership, proposing that true leaders do not make other people into followers but into other leaders. The qualities of such leaders were courage, endurance, patience, humor, flexibility, resourcefulness, along with the abiltiy to keep a cool head even when things were going badly. The type of leaders who attract large crowds of followers were more likely to enslave people than make them into other confident leaders.

Holt gave his view that higher education in the USA had limited value. It is possible to do interesting and useful work without college degrees. It can be hard, but it is also hard with a college degree since most of those who get degrees do not end up with work that is worthwhile and fulfilling. Ironically, they often end up with work that used to be done by people without degrees. If people want to go to college for the sport and social facilities, that is fine, but we do not have to pretend that anyone necessarily learns anything very important in such places.

The second issue ends with notes on the wide variety of reasons for taking children out of school. Some do so because schools are too competitive, some because they are too socialistic; some because they teach too much religion, others because they do not teach enough; some because they see the curriculum as fragmented, dull and irrelevant, whereas others like the curriculum but do not feel it is taught well enough. What was important was not to get agreement on these issues but to support each other in the right to educate at home in the ways each family thought best.

But the third edition signals a new emphasis. There was more material and correspondence about legal matters than anything else. Families wishing to educate at home were often encountering threats rather than intelligent questions, sympathy or support. Although lawyers could be useful at some stage, much of the basic research would have to be done by the families themselves. GWS would be used to report useful findings.

In addition, later issues contained model letters to send to education authorities and a list of questions about schools in the locality. Since schools and the authorities seemed to be claiming the right to judge home-based education programs, issue 4 of GWS contained a searching list of questions to ask about the local school system.

One legal ruling reported in GWS number 9 was about equivalence. It listed ways in which home-based education could not be compared to schools, including a significant difference in learning methods. One-to-one informal learning through purposive conversation was common in homes but rare in schools, where the 'stand and deliver' method of teaching was the normal approach. Standardized tests were also seen as of less importance in the home situation. Such reports were invaluable to newcomers in negotiation with the authorities. GWS number 10 proposed that when writing up home-education plans, it had become necessary to quote legal material wherever possible.

GWS commented from time to time on differences among home-based educating families and urged tolerance and solidarity on the basic right to educate at home. But in issue 10 a useful list of differences on key values within the school system was published:

A classroom in which children are expected to compete with each other is very different from one in which competitions arise naturally and spontaneously from the cooperative life of the group.

A classroom which measures children against each other or against outside standards is very different from one in which each child is encouraged to assess himself.

A classroom in which children learn by doing is very different from one in which they learn by being told.

A classroom in which the work is fed to children in tiny sequential bites is very different from one in which children tackle problems in full and life-like complexity.

A classroom in which children share significantly in planning what happens to them is very different from one in which things are planned

for them, and both are different from a classroom where children run
the show.

A classroom that encourages self-discipline is very different from one in
which the teacher disciplines. Both are different from a classroom artfully
regulated by rewards.

GWS continued for 16 years after John Holt's death. It closed in November
2001 with issue number 143. Holt Associates, Patrick Farenga, Susannah
Sheffer, Meredith Collins, Ginger Fitzsimmons and Mary Maher continued
to publish GWS using the money from Holt's estate, but eventually the
money ran out and closure was seen as inevitable.

Part 3

The Reception and Influence of John Holt's Work

Chapter 14

The Home-Based Education Movement

Readers will find that some of the material in this chapter revisits ideas explored in Chapters 11 and 13. The purpose of this chapter, however, is to feature the work of Holt on the credibility of home-based education as a significant contribution to recent educational thinking.

As was noted earlier, Holt's relationship with teachers was, at first, positive. In his first book, he wrote about classrooms and what he thought might be done to make them more effective learning environments. So, he appeared to be on teachers' side. But when he began to write and lecture about the need to go way beyond such damage limitation and recycle schools into learner-managed places, he gradually lost their sympathy. Teachers, he began to conclude, were not brave enough to engage in radical changes. At an early stage, he believed that perhaps three-quarters of teachers were in agreement with him. Later, he thought it might be half. Even later, he thought it might be a quarter. In the end, when he was writing his most radical books, he concluded it was more like 2 or even 1 per cent. He also developed a low opinion of teachers because of their origins low down the social order, which led them to put a premium on conserving the status quo. Their emphasis on the status quo produced too many dull teachers who were inclined to overrate order, very concerned about their own authority and status, convinced that a message of 'study hard and you can be like me' had wide appeal to the young. So, Holt argued, what could an appeal to give children more freedom mean to such teachers, who had never been very free themselves? He concluded that city schools fail because they have many such teachers.

As it turned out, his most fervent supporters turned out to be parents, and when he realized this he began to work with the emerging home-based education movement, referred to in the USA as homeschooling. His book on the subject was entitled *Teach Your Own* and was published in 1981. In it, Holt set out the case for home-based education. Next, he set out to report on the wealth of experience of those who were taking this path. Third, he intended the book to be a manual for action and inspiration for those just setting out. A particular feature was information about the legal situation in various American states.

Teach Your Own was a little misleading as a title, since Holt had dismissed most teaching as anti-educational. But this book was meant for parents, and in any case he had allowed two exceptions in the case of teaching. One was teaching that taught you how to become a better self-teacher, and the other was 'invited' teaching.

The bleak attitudes of fatalism that Holt encountered in most teachers and parents were not shared by those who took on the responsibility of home-based education. The fatalistic view was that the world was an unjust and often unpleasant place and that it was not going to change for the better. In addition, people holding such a view had developed faith in violence, whether physical or psychological, as a way to solve problems, despite the evidence of its failure. John Holt concluded that while such parents were in a majority, any general movement for school reform was doomed, so it would be more worthwhile to work with the homeschoolers.

To support parents who had begun to educate their children at home, John Holt and his associates established a service organization that they called Growing Without Schooling, as was mentioned in Chapter 11. From now on, home-based education, or homeschooling, became the focus of his writing and activity. His work, and the work of many others, has borne fruit. In 1994, it was estimated that over one million families in the USA were engaged in home-based education, and a higher figure of one and a half million has been suggested. Home-based education in the USA has its own research journal, edited by Brian Ray, its own publishing house, and a considerable range of commercial publications and services.

Why people choose home-based education

As was discussed in Chapter 11, Holt identifies three main reasons why people take on home-based education. (Others have listed as many as ten reasons.) Top of the list is that they want to stop their children from being unnecessarily hurt by school, whether mentally, spiritually or physically. A second is that the parents enjoy being with their children while watching and helping them learn: they do not want to give this up to complete strangers called teachers. Third, some families decide that raising children is their business and not that of the government. All kinds of people can and do home-educate for one or more of the above reasons plus several others. The number of people involved, however, remains a matter of intelligent guesswork rather than complete accuracy.

Who chooses home-based education?

Personally, I have found people quick to construct, from guesswork, stereotypes of families opting for home-based education. They usually start by assuming that the people concerned are well-off or even rich people. Holt confirms my own experience that this is false:

> We have had almost no correspondence with people who, judging by their addresses, writing paper, businesses, etc., were obviously rich. Most families who write to us have incomes well below the national average. (*Teach Your Own*, p. 14)

This is confirmed by recent studies in the UK such as *The Face of Home-Based Education* by Mike Fortune-Wood (Nottingham: Educational Heretics Press, 2005).

Holt goes on to say that homeschoolers often appear as average in everything – except stubbornness, courage, independence, and trust in themselves and their children. They have also become critical of what schools are actually like and what they achieve, both in general and, often by hard experience, for their children in particular.

A few follow Holt himself and go on to question the notion of compulsory schooling as a serious infringement of civil liberties. Holt's list of ten ways in which the civil liberties of children are violated, including secret record keeping and testing by compulsion, was given in Chapter 11. Protecting children from harm can range from bullying at school to the experience of families who see alert, lively-minded children become subdued and lose their sparkle and their smiles after starting school. Taking the children out of school is seen as damage limitation before a kind of healing can take place. Finding that home-based education is a superior form of education often comes later, and the initial negative motivation of just stopping damage gives way to positive celebration of the virtues of home-based education.

The social life: a gain in quality

Often, the first question that people ask, when startled by the news that some people prefer home-based education, concerns socialization. People imagine that if children are taught at home, they miss the valuable social life of the school. This question was discussed in Chapter 11. Holt points out that in fact the poor quality of the social life is often the reason why people pull their children out of school (see page 112).

Home-based education is more hopeful. The kinds of schools we have now are set up to divide people into winners and losers, and prepare young people for a lifetime of winning or losing, where the losers are then fated to look for others to look down on to make themselves feel a bit better. By contrast, most children who learn without school, or who go only when they want to, grow up with a much stronger sense of their own dignity and worth, and therefore with much less need to despise and hate others. Thus, such people may be able to afford to be kind, patient, generous, forgiving and tolerant as a consequence of being people who are secure in having love and respect for themselves, and therefore have energy and concern that they can devote to others (*Teach Your Own*, p. 37).

'Social mixing'

Another objection to home-based education, also discussed in Chapter 11 (page 111), is that of the 'social mixing' schools claim to provide. But, in fact, Holt observes, children spend most of their school hours in the same group of the same age, and since most schools eventually stream or set children for examination purposes, the experience of different people narrows as they get older. While the schooled are locked into the company of each other for 15,000 hours or more of their young lives, the home-educated are often out and about in society mixing with all kinds of people, thereby gaining in social experience, social skills and independence.

Parents with narrow visions

Another, and much more difficult, question is that of parents with narrow visions. As we saw on page 43, Holt starts from the proposition that in a free country, as long as you obey the law you can believe what you like. Schools act as if it is clear what ideas should be taught and which should be frowned on as narrow or bigoted, but who is to say which set of ideas should be imposed? Moreover, schools do not seem to be any good at actually changing negative attitudes. Newspapers and television show that there is plenty of prejudice left. What schools can be good at is confirming certain attitudes. Holt gives the example of a journalist friend who spent time in schools to find out what values young people were mostly concerned about, and found that it was money, sex and drugs rather than building a better world. Whatever effort schools put into resisting the values of the commercial culture seems to have been unsuccessful.

'Unqualified' parents

The fact that parents are not qualified teachers is another protest raised against Holt's ideas. In dealing with this question, Holt sets out to demystify teaching and learning. Humans have been sharing information and skills with the young for centuries using a few simple commonsense ideas, Holt says (see the quotation on page 112). Parents using these principles, Holt declares, can cope as well as, if not better than, any certified teacher, and, as we saw earlier, Holt notes a court case in Kentucky where the verdict given was that there was no evidence that certificated teachers produced better results. As was noted in Chapter 11, there are other advantages to students learning at home: their parents are not distracted by the problems of managing a class; they know the children better, including their spoken and unspoken signals; and they care more about them – they are not teaching in order to earn a salary. Also, parents are not bound by the limiting knowledge formulas of school.

Parents can also use a more effective learning method than formal instruction: purposive conversation. Studies have shown that we remember about 10 per cent after formal instruction, but 50 per cent after purposive conversation (Meighan, 2005).

But parents who offer their children the chance to have a home-based education do need 'qualifications' other than teacher certification. The quotation from Holt's *Teach Your Own* reproduced on page 113 explains what he thought were the attitudes needed. Few parents start out with *all* these qualities, but by trial and error they gain or strengthen them along the way. But most will have exercised many of these attributes in bringing up their young children in their early years, so they are not outside their capabilities or experience.

The politics of home-based education

Social change occurs when people change their lives, rather than their political parties or political beliefs (page 114). Thus, Holt decided to seek out people who were prepared to speak out in order to change things. He wanted to encourage true leaders, those who make us think, 'If they can do that . . . I can do it too.' Such leaders do not make people into followers, but into new leaders. Consequently, Holt argues, in the movement for home-based education, everyone becomes a leader.

Abandoning schools

There are those who argue that parents should stay with schools and try to make them better. But Holt came to conclude that schools were not a good idea gone wrong , but a bad idea from the outset.

The practicalities: how to opt out of schooling

Holt and his associates in Growing Without Schooling provided practical advice for parents on how to get started. This included ideas for preparing their letters and documents for schools and education authorities (see pages 136–7). As we have seen, many families reported that *making the decision* to opt out of schooling turns out to be the most difficult part of homeschooling. Preparing the letters and then getting their learning adventure going turn out to be much more straightforward than they expected.

Learning difficulties

As we saw earlier, dyslexia and problems with left and right identification are two of the learning difficulties explored by Holt. His experience as a teacher and his reflections on that experience led him to argue that learning difficulties are usually created, or at least amplified, by the school. The question of special needs is investigated in Mike Fortune-Wood's book published in the UK, *The Face of Home-Based Education 2: Numbers, Support, Special Needs* (Nottingham: Educational Heretics Press, 2006).

Findings of the courts and legal strategies

Home-based education has been the subject of many court actions in the USA. Although the detailed findings are specific to US law, the general findings are of general interest, and were listed in Chapter 11.

In *Growing Without Schooling*, Holt and his associates advise parents to resist attempts to have their children measured by standardized tests. Making small concessions about the curriculum may be tolerated for the sake of harmony, but no concessions should be made over tests. The reason is that even in the narrow area that they cover, the tests do not measure well what they claim to measure; and furthermore, the tests do not touch those many areas outside the narrow school curriculum in which children may be learning a great deal. Testing leads, inevitably, to 'trading for grades'.

Advice to schools

Schools do not need to panic, for even with full school cooperation and support, Holt estimates that the number of homeschooled is not likely to exceed 10 per cent of the schooled population (see page 119), because people want children to be out of the way during the daytime, and governments support this attitude by encouraging both parents to work.

The main reason schools should cooperate with homeschooling is to learn from the experience of the families and how they get such good results. Holt's remarks on what schools have to learn are quoted on page 119.

As regards teacher education, Holt proposes that a spell working with a homeschooling family would be very stimulating for students and teachers who choose it. This has been tried out in the UK at Birmingham University, when it proved to be of benefit to both parties (see Roland Meighan, *Learning Unlimited*, Nottingham: Educational Heretics Press, 2001).

Part 4

The Relevance of Holt's Work Today

Chapter 15

Personalized Learning

'Personalized learning' has become a focus of recent UK government interest. The version that is attractive to advocates within the school-based learning system is heavily teacher controlled and can be caricatured as 'the teacher devises an individual's learning program, which can look very much like that of everybody else, and the learner signs it'.

The version devised independently of the advocates of school-based learning systems, by groups such as the Centre for Personalised Education Trust, based in the UK, is more radical: (see http://c.person.ed.gn.apc.org). The influence of John Holt is evident in the list of key vocabulary and concepts that follows:

Personalized education/learning – *key vocabulary and concepts*

- *Learner-managed learning* instead of teacher or government-managed learning.
- *The catalog curriculum* instead of the National Curriculum.
- *'Invited' teaching* instead of 'uninvited' teaching.
- Main method of *purposive conversation* instead of formal instruction.
- *Teachers* as 'the guide on the side' instead of 'the sage on the stage'.
- *Others* as encouragers and supporters instead of decision makers.
- The *learner as researcher* instead of passive receiver.
- A *democratic value system* instead of domination by others or 'anything goes'.
- *Non-ageist learning* in a local community learning center instead of Key Stages in a day prison.
- *Review and celebration of learning* instead of imposed testing.
- *Leadership as self-leadership* ('good leaders are rare, so I am following myself') instead of appointed authoritarian leaders.

- *Discipline is self-discipline*; also, cooperation with others instead of having 'miserable rule-followers' forced to obey orders and rules imposed by others.
- *Assessment and certification only at the request of learners* instead of imposed assessment.
- *Personal learning plans* devised from the needs, concerns, interests of the learner instead of Key Stages (or 'Standards', as they were called in the first National Curriculum for England and Wales).
- *Education* is 'asking questions all the time' and going on to question the questions, instead of learning the official questions and official answers.
- *Schools* need to become invitational all-age 'voluntary associations of seekers after truth'.

The significance of John Holt's work is seen in such a list. Almost all of these features were articulated in his work, and others were implied.

Learner-managed learning

As regards learner-managed learning instead of teacher- or government-managed learning, Holt maintained that the case for traditional authoritarian education as found in schools was weak, and was getting ever weaker. In a rapidly changing world, the case for an education that will give a child primarily resourcefulness, flexibility, curiosity, skill in learning and readiness to unlearn, instead of knowledge and certainty, grows stronger year by year (*The Underachieving School*, p. 155). Furthermore, he proposed that we need an education that aims to produce people who have no wish to do harm. Traditional education, far from ever solving this problem, has never tried to solve it, he argued. Indeed, its efforts have, if anything, been to achieve the opposite. A significant aim of traditional education had always been to make children into the kind of adults who were competitive rather than cooperative, and ready to hate and kill anyone their leaders might declare to be their enemies (*The Underachieving School*, p. 98).

But the way *we* learn best is the same as the way children learn best, Holt observed. Let me repeat a passage already quoted:

> We learn best when we, not others, are deciding what we are going to try to learn, and when, and how, and for what reasons or purposes; when we, not others, are in the end choosing people, materials, and experiences from which and with which we will be learning; when we, not others, are judging how easily or quickly or well we are learning, and when we have learned enough; and above all when we feel the wholeness and openness

of the world around us, and our own freedom and power and competence in it. (*What Do I Do Monday?*, p. 95)

The catalog curriculum

Most of our current assumptions about adults planning schooling in order to work *on* children rather than *with* children are just plain wrong, Holt concluded. He wrote that he did not believe in the curriculum, in grades, in teacher-judged learning. Instead, he believed in children learning, with the assistance and encouragement of adults, the things they want to learn, when they want to learn them, how they want to learn them, why they want to learn them (*The Underachieving School*, p. 146). The notion of the catalog curriculum is implied here, for children should have access to the whole range of learning possibilities, experiences and ideas.

Teaching only if invited instead of uninvited instruction

Holt wrote that he learned in his experience that uninvited teaching does not produce much learning of value, and for the most part such teaching prevents learning, not least by creating dependent learners (*Learning All the Time*, p. 128).

Purposive conversation instead of formal instruction

Holt does not use the term 'purposive conversation', but it is implied in several of his books, where he reports conversations with children stimulated by their questions. He proposed a hard doctrine for those wishing to help children learn: 'no question, no teaching'.

Teachers as 'guides on the side', not 'sages on stages'

The idea of providing encouragement and support as children set about their chosen learning activities also applied to the task of teachers. Holt admitted he had been at fault himself in this respect, as he painfully learned that effective learning is only rarely the product of imposed teaching. He wrote that he was an ingenious and resourceful teacher, clever about thinking up lesson plans and demonstrations and motivating devices. Slowly and painfully, he learned that when he started teaching less, 'the children started learning more'. He could sum up in five to seven words what he eventually learned as a teacher. The seven-word version was that 'learning was not the product of teaching'. The five-word version was 'teaching does not make learning'. Organized education operated 'on the assumption that children learn only when and only what and only because we teach them'. This was not true and was 'close to one hundred per cent false' (*Learning All the Time*, p. 160). Holt's definition of the good teacher was encapsulated in the words 'What we can best learn from good teachers is how to teach ourselves better' (*Never Too Late*, p. 2).

Others as encouragers and supporters, not decision makers

Adults can best help by making more and more of the world accessible and available to children. The key word, Holt wrote, was access: to people, places, experiences, workplaces, cities, countries, streets, buildings, while making available tools, books, records, toys and any other resources (*Learning All the Time*, p. 127).

Learners as researchers instead of passive receivers

The last published book of John Holt, *Learning All the Time*, takes up the theme of learners as researchers. Here he shares his experience and observations that healthy children are curious and eager to explore the world and do not have to be motivated, unless insensitive adults have already damaged or weakened this natural urge to learn. Children are passionately eager to make as much sense as they can of the world around them. Moreover, they are extremely good at it, and do it as scientists do, by creating knowledge out of experience. Children, he notes, are acting like scientists all the time, which is to say looking, noticing, wondering, theorizing, testing their theories, and changing them as often as they have to (*Learning All the Time*, p. 134).

Democratic value system instead of domination by others, or 'anything goes'

Custodial-type schools cannot teach democratic morality, only domination and submission, which is why they are favored by totalitarian regimes. To talk of using the schools to teach morality, Holt saw as a bad joke. We might as well talk of using the army to teach pacifism. He quoted Edgar Friedenberg where he says that powerlessness corrupts. The schools, by taking the power to make choices from their students, corrupt them (*Instead of Education*, p. 191).

Elsewhere, Holt wrote of the fine talk among educators about democratic values when what was really going on was a long-drawn-out course in 'practical slavery', and mean-spirited competition against other children having precedence over cooperation (*The Underachieving School*, p. 25).

Non-ageist learning

We may assume that Holt would have approved of the idea of non-ageist learning in a local community learning center instead of age-defined learning in a national chain of day prisons. In his book *Never Too Late*, Holt attacks the idea of age-related learning with some vigor, using his own experience of learning to play the cello later in life – something regarded as almost impossible by the rigid minds of the music establishment. But he also takes on the idea in *Freedom and Beyond* (p. 117), where he conducts an imaginary conversation with someone on another planet, asking them where their schools are to be found. The person wanted to know what Holt meant by a school. He is puzzled by the answer of special places where children go to learn things at the direction of special people. 'But people learn things everywhere from anyone on our planet", is the reply, and the other planet dweller was puzzled by the idea that you need special places and special people to do this at special ages. Holt gives up trying to explain the Earth-bound system.

Review and celebration of learning instead of imposed testing

Imposed testing subverts education, Holt declares, for it seems clear that the greater the threat posed by a test, the less it can measure, far less encourage, learning. There are several reasons for this, but one of the most important is that whenever students know they are being judged by the results of tests, they turn their attention from the material to the tester. What becomes paramount 'is not the course or its meaning to the student', but whatever can be deduced 'is in the tester's mind'. 'Learning becomes less a search for any truth than a battle of wits.' The testers are no longer guides and helpers, but a kind of enemy (*The Underachieving School*, p. 53).

Leadership as self-leadership instead of appointed authoritarian leaders

'Good leaders are rare, so I am following myself', says one slogan on leadership. Holt agrees. Authoritarian leaders seek to create followers. The leaders Holt favors make us think that if others can do it, so can we, and so make people into new leaders, not followers. Such leaders create independence, not dependence (*Teach Your Own*, p. 68).

Discipline is self-discipline

Discipline is self-discipline, and also cooperation with others instead of the discipline of 'miserable rule-followers' forced to obey orders and rules imposed by others. In *Freedom and Beyond* (p. 100), Holt compares the standard authoritarian version of discipline of 'you will do it our way – or else' with the virtues of self-discipline and of cooperation with others, working to agreed rules.

Assessment and certification only at the request of learners instead of imposed assessment

Holt wrote that he was often asked if he would be happy to be operated on by doctors who had no qualifications. He would say he would not be, and disputed the interpretation that he was against assessment and certification. But such courses should be available when the learners decided to pursue them, and not form part of a coercive system (*Freedom and Beyond*, p. 196).

Personal learning plans

Holt never used the term 'personal learning plans' to my knowledge, but his whole approach was that of learners managing their own learning, an idea that is found in several of his books but receives particular attention in his last book, *Learning All the Time*. He would have argued that personal learning plans should be devised from the needs, concerns, interests of the learner instead of Key Stages (or 'Standards' as they were called in the first English and Welsh National Curriculum).

Education is 'asking questions all the time'

It should be clear from what we have seen of Holt's ideas that he favored the view that education is 'asking questions all the time', and going on to question the questions, instead of learning the official questions and official answers. By the time Holt wrote his book *Instead of Education*, he had taken up a stance against education as purveyed in schools: 'Meanwhile education – compulsory schooling – is a tyranny and a crime against the human mind and spirit. Let all those escape it who can, any way they can' (p. 226).

Voluntary associations

The idea that schools need to be recycled into invitational all-age 'voluntary associations of seekers after truth' is very much in line with Holt's views. For a time, schools were just that. In ancient times, when scholars (or 'schoolers') such as Peter Abelard visited a town, people of all ages would gather to discuss ideas with the visiting celebrity. What we have now, national chains of day prisons for the young, is an idea that came later. It is an idea a long way removed from the concept of a voluntary truth-seeking activity. In *Instead of Education*, Holt wrote extensively about the need to dismantle our oppressive schooling system and replace it with more intelligent arrangements for learning.

Conclusion

For a time, it looked as if the ideas of Holt, and others like Reimer, Illich, Goodman and Kohl, had been seen off by the regressive forces in society. But as the list above suggests, they are implict in the current considerations of the nature of personalized learning.

At times, Holt was pessimistic about the future. He thought schools would get worse rather than better. Schools could not change society, but, on a more optimistic note, he wrote that we can reconstruct learning if we want to: 'Schools are not a force of nature. People made them, thinking they would be useful; people can do away with them when they are no longer of any use' (*Instead of Education*, p. 213).

Bibliography

Editions of the books by John Holt quoted in this volume

How Children Fail (1969) Harmondsworth: Penguin Books
How Children Learn (1970) Harmondsworth: Penguin Books
What Do I Do Monday? (1970) New York: E.P. Dutton
The Underachieving School (1971) Harmondsworth: Penguin Books
Freedom and Beyond (1972) New York: E.P. Dutton
Escape from Childhood (1975) Harmondsworth: Penguin Books
Instead of Education (1977) Harmondsworth: Penguin Books
Teach Your Own (1981) Liss, Hampshire: Lighthouse Books
Learning All the Time (1991) Ticknall: Education Now, and Liss, Hampshire:
  Lighthouse Books (joint publication)
Never Too Late (1992) Ticknall: Education Now, and Liss, Hampshire: Light-
  house Books (joint publication)

Revised editions

Revised editions of both *How Children Fail* and *How Children Learn* were
published by Penguin Books in 1984. In them, John Holt adds passages
that record his later reflections on his earlier work. Most of these ideas are
found in his later books, as presented in this volume. I have not, therefore,
produced any separate notes on these two revised works.

Selected references

Goodman, P. (1971) *Compulsory Miseducation*, Harmondsworth: Penguin.
Harber, C. (2004) *Schooling as Violence*, London: Routledge.
Illich, I. (1971) *Deschooling Society*, London: Calder and Boyars.

Kohl, H. (1970) *The Open Classroom*, London: Methuen (US publication 1969).

Meighan, R. (2005) *Comparing Learning Systems*, Nottingham: Educational Heretics Press.

Postman, N. and Weingartner, C. (1971) *Teaching as a Subversive Activity*, Harmondsworth: Penguin (US publication 1969).

Reimer, E. (1971) *School Is Dead*, Harmondsworth: Penguin.

Shute, C. (1998) *Edmond Holmes and 'The Tragedy of Education'*, Nottingham: Educational Heretics Press.

Taylor-Gatto, J. (2003) *The Underground History of American Education*, New York: Oxford Village Press.

Index